D0847652

George Noory's
LATE-NIGHT SNACKS

George Noory's
LATE-NIGHT
SNACKS

Winning Recipes for Late-Night
Radio Listening

George Noory
and
William J. Birnes

A TOM DOHERTY ASSOCIATES BOOK
NEW YORK

A Forge Book
Published by Tom Doherty Associates, LLC
175 Fifth Avenue
New York, NY 10010

www.tor-forge.com

Forge® is a registered trademark of Tom Doherty Associates, LLC.

Library of Congress Cataloging-in-Publication data
is available upon request.

ISBN 978-0-7653-1408-6 (hardcover)
ISBN 978-1-4668-3364-7 (e-book)

Forge books may be purchased for educational, business, or promotional use.
For information on bulk purchases, please contact Macmillan Corporate and
Premium Sales Department at 1-800-221-7945, extension 5442,
or write specialmarkets@macmillan.com.

First Edition: November 2013

Printed in the United States of America

0 9 8 7 6 5 4 3 2 1

I'd like to thank and dedicate this book to my mother,
Georgette, who sees the light all the time.
—GEORGE NOORY

Dedicated to Nancy Hayfield
—WILLIAM J. BIRNES

Acknowledgments

We acknowledge with deep appreciation our *Coast to Coast AM* listening audience, the enthusiasts, the true believers, and the skeptics, without whose support over the years there wouldn't be a place where alternative theories of creation and human history could be discussed. These recipes are for you.

And to the efforts of our tireless editor, Kelly Quinn, whose insistence on doing things right keeps us honest.

Contents

George Noory's
LATE-NIGHT SNACKS

Introduction

Whether it's the planet with two suns and the coming disclosure of life in pools of water beneath the Martian surface, the secrets of the JFK assassination, or a remote-viewing session revealing artificial structures on the moon, as the talk gets more exciting, my listeners tell me they invariably get attacks of the munchies.

It's two in the morning in Los Angeles and only a few cars are on the 405, while on the East Coast the diners haven't yet opened for the morning rush. It's too late for dinner, too early for breakfast, but you're hungry and there's no pre-packaged, nuke-it-up fast food in the freezer. What can you find to eat?

Here's my answer. I've put together the ultimate in late-night treat cookbooks: *Late-Night Snacks*. Here are my own personalized recipes for the nighthawks and night owls transfixed by stories of the paranormal, UFOs, past lives, ghosts, and anything from ETs to poltergeists who go bump in the night. Whether you're hearing an interview from the late Father Malachi Martin on exorcism or revelations about remote viewing from Major Paul H. Smith, when your tension begins to rise and you have to have something to eat, my new cookbook is the place to turn.

So pick out your favorite recipes, gather all the ingredients, and keep them at the ready for when the pangs of hunger strike and you don't want to miss one word of my interviews. As your server says as he or she brings your gourmet dinner in the fine restaurant where you like to dine, "Enjoy."

1

• ALTERNATIVE HISTORY • CONSPIRACIES •

Toaster Tarts
Fast Microwaved Nachos
Savory Buttered Bread Sticks
Dumplings Love You
Secret Door Meat Loaf
Hearty Stew Over Rice in a Minute
Basic Tomato Sauce
Biscuit Baking Mix
Quick Biscuit Shortcake
Producer Tom's Midnight Popcorn Munchies
Rum Coffee for Your Nerves
Creamy Hot Cocoa for Your Soul

The world is a scary place, and it's hard to know who to trust. However, you can trust these recipes. Trust me on that.

I listen to all kinds of alternative narratives when it comes to history, and I always find them fascinating. After all, so much of what ends up in our history books is the product of consensus reasoning, and it doesn't cover all the bases. Some of the alternate views of history—from the Ancient Astronauts theory to Nibiru and beyond—are way out there, and some of them make good sense.

Then there are those nights when we have one of my favorite topics up for discussion: conspiracies. Again, I like to suspend disbelief while the author or researcher spins his tale. Wouldn't it be keen if the world really were being run by a hidden hand? That's such a comforting thought, and it's the reason I've grouped the following recipes together: they all make you feel comforted, as if Big Brother is giving you a big bear hug.

I've laid out an entire comfort meal for you for one perfect day. Keep to the other side of the room when you microwave, and don't worry about the ingredients in your normal fast food. Nothing to worry about.

We finish out the chapter with Producer Tom's Midnight Popcorn Munchies. That's how he selects the guests for the show: reading resumes at midnight, with popcorn, enjoying the three-ring circus. Three rings? Hmmmmm.

Toaster Tarts

Everything about toaster tarts is comfy. The toaster, our little workhorse of the morning, just does all the work for you, provided you put in some prep time the night before. Better yet, make a batch of these and pop them in the freezer for a great breakfast on the run that still feels special.

Yes, you can buy them packaged in the supermarket, but think of the mystery ingredients! And think of the fun of making them yourself in a variety of flavors, having them fresh, and saving money in the bargain.

Make these tarts in any of the many flavors that are available to tempt your children at breakfast (but you're really tempting yourself) in strawberry, blueberry, chocolate, peanut butter, cashew or almond butter and jelly, or apple.

TARTS
¾ cup vegetable shortening
¾ cup sugar
3 large eggs
3¾ cups all-purpose flour
3 teaspoons baking powder
½ cup strawberry preserves or Freezer Fruit
    Preserves (page 60)
1 egg yolk beaten with 2 tablespoons light cream

FROSTING
½ teaspoon Vanilla Bean Extract (page 205)
2 tablespoons whole milk
½ cup confectioners' sugar

1. Preheat the oven to 350°F. Grease a baking sheet.

Toaster Tarts

2. In the bowl of an electric mixer or in a food processor, cream together the shortening and sugar. Beat in the eggs, one at a time.

3. Sift the flour and baking powder into a bowl and stir into the shortening mixture to make a soft dough. Chill for 1 hour.

4. Turn the dough out onto a floured surface and roll out into twelve 8 by 12-inch rectangles.

5. Spread about a tablespoon of the preserves over half of each rectangle, staying well within the edges of the pastry. Fold the pastry dough over the preserves and trim the edges with a pastry wheel, or crimp with a fork to seal.

6. Place the tarts on the prepared baking sheet and brush with the egg yolk–cream mixture. Bake for 20 minutes. Set aside to cool.

7. Stir the vanilla and milk into the confectioners' sugar until you have a thin frosting. Dribble a tablespoon onto the top of each tart, or brush the frosting on using a pastry brush.

8. Wrap the tarts in aluminum foil and store in the refrigerator. The tarts will keep for about 7 days or can be frozen for 3 to 4 months.

TO USE   Unwrap a tart and place it in the toaster or toaster oven for 2 minutes if refrigerated and for 4 minutes if frozen. Or, unwrap a tart and cook it in the microwave for 1 minute on high if it has been refrigerated or for 2 minutes on high if it has been frozen. Be careful of the frosting, which gets extremely hot and somewhat runny when it is microwaved.

Makes 12 toaster tarts

VARIATIONS   Try adding coconut and chopped nuts to the filling, and sprinkle the frosting with ground cinnamon.

Add raisins, dates, and chopped nuts to a sliced apple filling. For a chocolate tart, try adding 1 tablespoon of Basic Chocolate Sauce (page 176) to the tart and topping it with frosting flavored with ¼ teaspoon orange extract.

Fast Microwaved Nachos

Here is your equally quick lunch, assuming you have a microwave nearby. Our listeners tend to be very busy during the day, so here is a fast hearty dish.

The trick to nachos is to use the right cheese. For me, it's a combination of Monterey Jack and cheddar cheese, both grated instead of sliced. They melt more easily that way. The other trick is to choose the right nacho chips. Again, for me, it's the restaurant-type chips, not strips.

You can add your favorite dishes on the side, such as chorizo sausage and guacamole, as well as salsa.

Spread your nacho chips out on a large plate that will fit in your microwave without getting caught if the tray rotates.

Generously sprinkle over the grated cheddar first and then the grated Jack cheese. Of course, as to whether your Jack cheese will contain jalapeños or anything else is up to you, but I like to add sliced fresh jalapeños right on top before I melt the cheese in the microwave.

Microwave for about 45 seconds on high, or until the cheese just begins to bubble. Let cool for just a bit to keep from burning your fingers on the plate, then carefully remove from the microwave. Depending on how many chips and how much cheese, you can serve anywhere from just yourself and a friend to an entire party.

Unless you don't feel like a party, of course. No one is judging. Eat them all by yourself.

VARIATIONS

◆ **Crushed Red Peppers:** To spice up your nachos the easy way, just before microwaving, shake some crushed red pepper flakes over the cheese. This will give your nachos a lot of snap depending on how much pepper you add.

◆ **Jalapeño Peppers:** If you like your nachos with fresh jalapeños covered with hot spicy cheese, wash and dice your jalapeños, pat dry, then spread over the nacho chips just before spreading the cheese. Add 15 seconds to the cooking time.

◆ **Chorizo Sausage:** You can prepare this in a variety of ways. My two favorites are with sausage on the side, easy enough, or with sausage scattered over the chips and cheese over the sausage, with or without jalapeños or with sweet bell peppers. The trick is to cook the sausage in advance. I like to boil the sausage for at least 15 minutes to make sure it's thoroughly cooked. Bring some water to a boil in a medium saucepan while you wash the sausage and then split the casings. When the water comes to a full boil, add the sausage and cook for 15 minutes. To test for doneness, split one of the sausages in two and see if it is cooked on the inside. If the meat is still pink, boil again for another 5 minutes and test again. When the sausage is done, remove from the boiling water, let cool for 5 minutes, dry, and then slice. Now you can fry the sausage briefly in garlic and oil, adding sweet bell peppers, jalapeños, and onions if you like. Begin by heating 1 teaspoon of olive oil and 2 garlic cloves in a frying pan. Slice a small green or red bell pepper and a small brown onion. When the garlic just starts to brown, add the sausage, peppers, and onion and brown thoroughly. Remove from the pan and transfer to a paper towel to drain. Scatter over the nachos, sprinkle with the cheese, and microwave for 1 minute.

◆ **Me Nachos Su Nachos:** If I want to make an entire meal out of what was once a snack, this is how I do it. I make a huge platter of meat and peppers nachos by frying ground beef and sausage together along with bell peppers and onions, sprinkling on some crushed red pepper flakes and even a little taco sauce, adding a pinch of dried oregano, and then cooking it in a conventional oven at 350°F for 25 minutes. Here are the steps: Preheat the oven to 350°F. While you boil the sausage in a medium saucepan, brown 1 pound of ground beef in a skillet with a tablespoon of oil and a garlic clove until thoroughly cooked. Drain, then keep warm over low heat. When the sausage is thoroughly cooked and no longer pink on the inside, cut it into small pieces and add to the simmering ground beef. Add the sliced or diced bell pepper and onion and cook until the pepper and onion begin to brown. Drain and then pour the mixture over the nacho chips. Cover the nachos with your favorite shredded cheese. Mine is a mixture of cheddar and Monterey Jack. Place in the oven and bake for 25 minutes. Serve hot.

Savory Buttered Bread Sticks

Now that you are home for the rest of the long evening, why not start your nibbling with some bread sticks? The Olive Garden is popular for a reason, you know. Not that anyone is following you.

This recipe is a good way to use day-old Italian or French bread because you can make it up, wrap it in aluminum foil, and freeze. When reheated, the bread tastes fresh again.

You can also vary the kinds of butter you use, from Garlic Butter (page 186) for the traditional garlic bread to French Herb Butter (page 187) for a light lunch with soup to Ooh-la-la Butter (page 192) for a sweet breakfast of quick French toast.

Additional variations follow the main recipe, and you will probably be inspired to invent more of your own.

If you are baking a loaf of Savory Buttered Bread that you have frozen, add 15 minutes to the baking time.

1 large loaf Italian or French bread
½ cup (1 stick) prepared butter, softened:
  Garlic Butter (page 186)
  French Herb Butter (page 187)
  Ooh-la-la Butter (page 192)

1. Preheat the oven to 400°F.
2. Slice the bread crosswise, leaving the bottom half in one piece.
3. Brush all of the butter along the cut sides of the bread, both top and bottom. Put the bread loaf back together and wrap tightly in aluminum foil.
4. Bake for 15 to 20 minutes. Cut the bread into 1 by 4-inch rectangles while it's still warm. Serve immediately.

Makes 1 loaf

VARIATION   For French bread, spread with Ooh-la-la Butter, as above, and instead of baking, dip the slices in 2 eggs scrambled with ¼ cup whole milk, seasoned with salt and pepper, and 2 teaspoons of sugar. Fry in butter, sprinkle with ground cinnamon, and serve with maple syrup or one of the Sweet Berry Syrups (page 203).

Dumplings Love You

Dumplings are old-fashioned, and yes, they are fattening, but nothing in the world is as comforting as seeing them sitting cozily on the top of stews, broth, or even chili. Try the pretty speckled ones for variety, or when you want to impress yourself.

Old-Fashioned Dumplings

> 2 cups Biscuit Baking Mix (page 29)
> 1 cup whole milk

In a medium bowl, stir the baking mix and milk together to form a soft dough.

TO USE   At the perfect moment, drop the dough by spoonfuls onto the top of stew, soup, or chili—it must be nearly ready to eat, and the liquid bubbling hot and gently simmering. Simmer for 10 minutes, then cover tightly and cook for 10 minutes more.

Herb Dumplings

> 2 cups Biscuit Baking Mix (page 29)
> 1 cup whole milk
> 1 tablespoon chopped fresh herbs: parsley, dill, or chives
> 1 garlic clove, minced
> 1 teaspoon freshly ground black pepper

Mix the dumpling dough and cook, as above.

Vegetable Dumplings

> 2 cups Biscuit Baking Mix (page 29)
> 1 cup whole milk
> 2 tablespoons finely chopped onion, green bell pepper, or scallions
> 1 teaspoon freshly ground black pepper

Mix and cook, as above.

Each recipe makes 12 dumplings

Secret Door Meat Loaf

This recipe has a secret ingredient that makes all the difference: pepperoni. No need to tell until the flavor introduces itself, just like a favorite guest on the secret door segment of *Coast*.

> 2 slices bread
> 2 large eggs, lightly beaten
> 1 teaspoon dried oregano
> 1 teaspoon garlic powder
> ¾ teaspoon salt
> 1 cup chopped mushrooms (you can use fresh shiitake mushrooms or simply open a can of mushroom pieces and stir them in)
> 1 cup shredded part-skim mozzarella cheese
> 2 tablespoons ketchup, plus more for basting (optional)
> ½ cup finely chopped pepperoni
> 1½ pounds ground beef

1. Preheat the oven to 350°F. Meanwhile, tear the bread into small pieces or quickly blend in a food processor until it forms fine crumbs—pieces or crumbs are both good.
2. In a large bowl, beat the eggs with the oregano, garlic powder, and salt.
3. Stir in the bread crumbs, mushrooms, cheese, ketchup, if using, and pepperoni.

4. Add the beef and work all the other ingredients into it. I use my hands for this.
5. Form the mixture into a 9 by 6-inch loaf and place it in a loaf pan. Bake for 45 minutes.
6. After 45 minutes of baking, brush the meat loaf with more ketchup, if desired. Cover and bake for 1 hour, or until the meat loaf is cooked through in the center.

Makes 1 meat loaf

Hearty Stew Over Rice in a Minute

I make no apologies for the simplicity of this recipe. In fact, it's more like a bowl of late-night convenience food, but it does the trick, it's quick, and it's satisfying.

The satisfaction level of this recipe is that you fill up on rice. I like rice. Always have. And sometimes late at night when I'm researching for a guest and I feel my energy flagging, I like to have a bowl of stew over rice to recharge myself. Here's one of my recipes, which you can make with rice you boil from scratch or with instant rice packets or even Minute Rice.

The great part about this recipe is that you can use any one of the great flavors of Campbell's Chunky Soup for beef stew, chicken stew, or even vegetable stew. Any way you like it, this is a filling snack or a full meal for a family on a busy winter's day.

¼ cup rice or single serving package of Minute
  Rice
One 10.75-ounce can Campbell's Chunky Soup
  (your favorite flavor)
Salt and freshly ground black pepper (optional)

1. To make a single serving of rice from scratch: In a small saucepan, bring ½ cup of water and a pinch of salt to a boil. When the water is at a rolling boil, add ¼ cup of your favorite rice, stir, and return to a boil. Reduce the heat to simmer and cover. Check the rice every 5 minutes or so until the water is absorbed and the rice is fluffy soft. Remove from the heat and fluff with a fork.

2. To make the rice using instant rice or Minute Rice: Follow the package directions. When the rice is fully cooked, fluff with a fork and set aside.

3. To make the stew: Choose either Campbell's Chunky Soup or any other thick, canned soup, and heat the soup in a saucepan or in the microwave until steaming hot. Pour over the cooked rice, and reheat in the microwave for 1 minute. Season to taste with salt and pepper.

VARIATION   If you don't have the time or inclination to boil up a serving of rice, just heat up a slice of thick French bread in the microwave for 15 seconds and pour the serving of Chunky Soup over the slice of bread. This makes a great open-faced stew sandwich that's just as satisfying.

Basic Tomato Sauce

Nothing is more comforting to the Italians I know than to have a whole lot of tomato sauce in the pantry. This recipe is an ideal way to use up all the bountiful tomatoes of summer, and if you make sauce in quantity when tomatoes are plentiful, the cost-per-unit savings can be enormous. The procedure described is how my friends' grandmothers always made her their sauces. This meatless version can be improved upon, made quicker still (Instant Pasta Primavera sauce, see variation on page 168), or made with a summer or Mexican flavor (Gazpacho-style Sauce, page 104).

2 garlic cloves, sliced
2 medium onions, chopped
2 small green bell peppers, seeded and chopped
2 teaspoons olive oil
Two 20-ounce cans Italian plum tomatoes
    (whole), or 4 pounds ripe plum or regular
    tomatoes
½ teaspoon salt
½ teaspoon freshly ground black pepper
½ teaspoon sugar
½ teaspoon dried basil or 2 to 3 fresh basil
    leaves, minced
½ teaspoon dried oregano
4 sprigs fresh parsley or ½ teaspoon dried parsley

1. In a large, heavy saucepan over medium-low heat, cook the garlic, onions, and bell peppers in the olive oil, stirring frequently, until the vegetables are soft and the onion is translucent, 5 to 8 minutes.
2. If using canned tomatoes, stir them into the oil mixture.
3. If using fresh tomatoes, put a separate pan of water on the stovetop to simmer while the vegetables are cooking. Drop in 3 or 4 tomatoes at a time, and transfer them after a minute or so to a bowl of cold water. As soon as the tomatoes are cool to the touch, peel each one over the pot containing the olive oil mixture, discard the peels, and drop in the whole tomato.
4. Add the salt, pepper, sugar, basil, oregano, and parsley. Simmer, covered, for about 1 hour. Taste and adjust the seasonings.
5. The sauce can be stored, covered, in the refrigerator for

about 1 week, or frozen for 3 to 9 months. Glass jars are better to use for storage than plastic, which reacts to the tomatoes over time.

NOTE   If you don't object to the tomato skins, or are using Italian plum tomatoes, peeling may not be necessary. However, if your sauce is intended for company, small children, or invalids, the tomatoes should be peeled.

Makes 32 ounces sauce

Biscuit Baking Mix

I've used this mix as the basis for several of the recipes that follow, so if you think you will be making lots of pancakes, shortcake, or biscuits in the near future, double or triple the quantity of the basic baking mix.

It keeps very well in the pantry and you can use it for a quick finish for a meat or vegetable casserole by simply sprinkling a few teaspoons of the mix on the top before baking—it will sink to the bottom and form a soft pie crust.

10 cups all-purpose flour
1 cup baking powder
1 tablespoon salt
2 cups shortening

1. Sift the dry ingredients together into a large bowl. Using two knives, a pastry blender, or your food processor, cut the shortening into the dry ingredients in the bowl. If mixing by hand, add the shortening in spoonfuls and cut it into the dry ingredients until the mixture has the texture of coarse cornmeal. If you are using a food processor, place the dry ingredients and shortening in the processor bowl (fitted with the metal blade) and pulse, starting and stopping often during processing and watching it closely until the mixture has the texture of coarse cornmeal.

2. Store the mix in a labeled, airtight container. It will keep on the pantry shelf for 1 to 6 months in dry weather. In very hot and humid weather, it's a good idea to keep the mix in the refrigerator.

Use the basic mix to make any of the following dinner or breakfast accompaniments:

- Quick Rolled Biscuits (page 232)
- Dumplings Love You (page 23)
- Crepes Diem (page 137)
- Quick Mabel, the Pancakes! (page 252)
- Surefire Waffles (page 227)

You can also use the mix to make these quick desserts:

- Quick Coffee Cake (page 113)
- Quick Biscuit Shortcake (below)

Makes 10 cups mix

Quick Biscuit Shortcake

I have found that the world seems to be evenly divided between those who like a biscuit-type shortcake and those who prefer a pound-cake type. Why debate the issue? Have both, especially when you're listening to Stan Friedman tee off on the skeptic of the month. Try this recipe, making sure you don't overcook it, before you commit yourself to the pound-cake version.

> 2 cups Biscuit Baking Mix (page 29)
> ½ cup whole milk
> 3 tablespoons butter, melted
> ¼ cup sugar

1. Preheat the oven to 400°F.
2. Mix together all of the ingredients, stirring until a soft dough forms. Turn out the dough onto a surface dusted with more of the baking mix or just plain flour and knead gently for 30 seconds.
3. Roll out the dough ½ inch thick and cut into squares or 3-inch rounds.
4. Bake on an ungreased baking sheet for 10 minutes, or until golden brown.

TO USE   Split the shortcakes in half horizontally, spoon berries or preserves between the halves and over the top, and finish off with sweetened heavy cream, whipped if you'd like.

Makes 6 shortcakes

Producer Tom's Midnight Popcorn Munchies

Still another variation on an old theme, this recipe can be specifically for you or your adult children friends. It's for folks who like to stay up late and listen to *Coast* to find out about the truth no one else will ever tell you.

A bowl of this popcorn is also a great accompaniment to an old movie, say a flying saucer movie from the 1950s. You know, the one that scared you when you were a kid, but now looks more like a greater truth than pure fiction, especially after you learned that the CIA fed flying saucer stories to the major studios so as to marginalize UFOs and the people who wrote about them. How do we know this? The CIA told us so in its own report.

Yes, these munchies are my producer's favorite. They are like snackin' jacks, but with just a twist to differentiate it and make it slightly more adult. If, as an adult, you want the mixture to be a little sweeter, use regular dry-roasted peanuts and unsalted, also called sweet, butter. If you want to add a bit of salty tang to the mixture, use salted butter instead of unsalted butter.

12 cups popped corn
1½ cups shelled roasted peanuts
½ cup honey
½ cup (1 stick) salted or unsalted butter, your
  choice

1. In a large bowl, mix together the popcorn and nuts, stirring, shaking, and tossing until they are thoroughly combined.
2. In a microwave-safe bowl, combine the honey and butter and warm in your microwave on medium for 3 minutes or on high for 90 seconds until the butter melts and is just starting to bubble. The mixture should be able to flow.
3. Pour the honey-butter mixture over the popcorn in the bowl and toss so that everything is thoroughly combined and coated.
4. Spread the mixture out in a microwave-safe pan and microwave on high for 4 minutes. Stir and rotate and then continue to microwave for another 4-minute cycle. Remove from the microwave and set aside until cool to the touch, and the brick has the consistency of peanut brittle.

5. Break the brick up into handy chunks before serving, wrapping up for a lunch box, or storing in an airtight container. This will keep on your shelf for 2 weeks, but it won't last that long. It will call to you like the sirens called to Odysseus as he was strapped to the mast. Unlike Odysseus, you will be unable to resist.

Makes about twelve 1-cup servings

VARIATIONS   Where is it written that you can only make this recipe with peanuts? Not here.

You can also use cashews, the saltier the better, or even walnuts or almonds. You know what? Why force yourself to choose, add all three with some peanuts and celebrate the variety.

Remember when you were a kid and you dug your teeth into that nougat-y candy with peanuts on top and maybe a hint or more of chocolate? Wanna get crazy? Try this—while the mixture is still warm, shape it into little rolls and then cut it. It will taste just like that old-time candy bar, but without the chocolate. Want the chocolate?

Take two pieces of dark chocolate and melt them just a little in a microwave-safe dish, and then roll your popcorn munchy in the chocolate to coat it. Eat too much of this and, if you're a chocoholic, you will drift off into a happy mellow reverie.

Rum Coffee for Your Nerves

This is an alternative to Spiced and Fancy After-Dinner Coffee (page 223) and is tasty on those bitter cold nights when the wind is howling about and you want to feel warm all over.

3 tablespoons honey, warmed slightly
1 cup heavy cream
3 cups freshly brewed coffee
1 pint vanilla ice cream
½ cup rum

1. Assemble all of the ingredients beforehand so that you can perform the steps in quick succession. Begin by stirring the honey into the heavy cream and setting the mixture aside.
2. Pour the hot coffee over the ice cream and stir in the honey-cream mixture. Add the rum and stir well. Serve immediately.

Makes 32 ounces coffee

Creamy Hot Cocoa for Your Soul

For the ultimate comfort food, just wrap your hands around a mug of hot cocoa. Now, let the conspiracies flow. You are safe in your own hovel.

Make up quantities of this mix in the nippy days of October and November, and you will always have a warm, nourishing drink on hand.

2 cups instant nonfat dry milk
¾ cup sugar
½ cup unsweetened cocoa powder
1 teaspoon salt
1 cup miniature marshmallows

Stir all of the ingredients together and store in a tightly closed jar or airtight container for up to 2 months.

TO USE   Put 2 to 3 heaping tablespoons of the mix into a mug and fill with boiling water or, for an extra-rich drink, hot milk. Top with whipped cream and sprinkle with ground cinnamon for a special treat.

Makes 20 ounces hot cocoa mix

2

• ALTERNATIVE MEDICINE • HEALTH •

Granny's Granola

Granola Rolls

Homemade Yogurt

Homemade Cream Cheese

Healthy Seed Treats

Healthy Bread Crumbs

Cheese Thins

Herby Vegetable Crackers

Fat-Free Faux Corn

Healthy Potato Chips

Peach Chutney

Presto Pesto

Micro Veggies

Turkey and Sprouts

Herbal Vinegar

Raspberry Vinegar

Apple Congee

Freezer Fruit Preserves

Frozen Fruiti Yogurt

Unadulterated Adult
Herbal Teas

As listeners to our show know full well, if you want to stay healthy, you are going to have to take matters into your own hands. The nastier additives in our food are not doing your body any good, so if you like to munch on happy snacks and tasty treats without worrying about your life span, you are in the right place.

The recipes that follow give you all of the flavor but none of the additives. Learn how to make your own granola, first of all, and with newfound strength from your own natural yogurt, move on to really healthy and unadulterated cheesies, crackers, and chutney.

Now you will need even less sleep, so tune in to the show tonight as you also fine-tune your body!

Granny's Granola

Let's start the ball rolling with the perfect start to any day. Or, the perfect end: consider this your go-to late-night solution to how to eat hearty and sleep peacefully.

4 cups old-fashioned rolled oats
1 cup wheat germ
½ cup instant nonfat dry milk
Any combination of the following ingredients to
    make a total of 4 more cups:
- Chopped nuts or sesame seeds
- Sunflower seeds or pumpkin seeds
- Dried fruit: raisins, apples, bananas, or dates
- ½ cup shredded unsweetened coconut
- 1 teaspoon ground cinnamon
- ½ cup vegetable oil or butter
- ½ to 1 cup honey
- 1 teaspoon Vanilla Bean Extract (page 205)

1. Preheat the oven to 350°F. Oil a shallow baking pan.
2. Combine the oats, wheat germ, dry milk, nuts, seeds, dried fruit, coconut, and cinnamon in a large bowl and stir thoroughly to combine.
3. In a small saucepan, heat the oil and honey slowly until they just begin to simmer. Remove from the heat and stir in the vanilla.
4. Stir the oil-honey mixture into the dry ingredients, making sure to coat all the dry ingredients well.
5. Turn the mixture out into the prepared pan and pat down well. Bake for 20 to 30 minutes. It's a good idea to check the granola every now and then to ensure that the top doesn't

brown too quickly. Stir carefully and pat down during the baking.

6. Remove from the oven and set aside to cool. When completely cool, store in a tightly covered jar or canister. If the weather is very warm or humid, store the granola in the refrigerator; otherwise, it will keep for about a month on the pantry shelf. Do not freeze.

Makes 11 cups granola

VARIATIONS   This recipe can be used as the basis for a crunchy, fruity candy by mixing the cereal with a bit of honey, forming into balls, rolling in Powdered Vanilla Sugar (page 180), and refrigerating.

Granola also makes an excellent topping for your homemade ice cream, pudding, and yogurt.

Granola Rolls

One of my favorite morning and lunchtime snacks has always been granola candies—bars, rolls, chocolate chip, peanut butter, raisin-nut-crunch versions. They travel well, and I love them all.

Here are recipes for these, and other varieties, all using your own lower-cost homemade granola. If you make these rolls up in quantity, you can refrigerate the extra ones, but don't try to freeze them or they will become soggy.

2½ cups Granny's Granola (page 39)
½ cup confectioners' sugar
½ cup light corn syrup

Granola Rolls

1. In a large bowl, mix together all of the ingredients.
2. When the granola is well moistened, shape the mixture into rolls, each about 1 inch in diameter.
3. Transfer the rolls to a baking sheet covered with wax paper or plastic wrap and refrigerate for 1 hour.
4. When chilled and firm, slice the rolls into individual-size pieces.
5. Store, wrapped in plastic wrap, in the refrigerator for 2 to 3 weeks.

Makes 25 ounces granola rolls

VARIATIONS   For a different flavor, add 1 cup of chocolate chips to the mixture, and press the mixture into a 9-inch-square cake pan. Chill in the refrigerator for 1 hour. Cut into squares when firm.

Or add 1 cup peanut butter to the mixture. Other additions might include 1 cup raisins, 1 cup nuts, or 1 cup peanut butter chips.

Try adding ½ cup honey and 1 teaspoon Vanilla Bean Extract (page 205) to the granola instead of confectioners' sugar.

Homemade Yogurt

Here is a late-night snack, a dessert, or even a quickie breakfast you can prepare well in advance to have on hand in your fridge whenever you want a healthy treat. If I'm listening to one of my fellow hosts on *Coast* and I want a fast pick-me-up, I can reach in and either have my homemade yogurt straight up or mixed with a spoonful of fruit preserves for something sweet.

To make yogurt, you must already have a bit of yogurt. You

will need yogurt with an active culture—Dannon is one of the best—but if you read the labels carefully, you're sure to find others. Then, after you've made your first batch, keep a small amount of your homemade yogurt plain and unflavored and ready to start the next batch.

A candy or kitchen thermometer is necessary for this recipe, at least the first time around, because yogurt making depends on bringing the milk to a favorable temperature for growing the yogurt culture. If you have a yogurt maker, by all means enjoy using it, but it isn't essential to yogurt making. Since there are several easy ways to keep the milk at the right temperature throughout the process, I've described some techniques here.

> **4 cups milk, 2 percent or low fat**
> **1 cup instant nonfat dry milk**
> **½ cup plain yogurt**

1. Heat the regular milk to 180°F. Check the temperature with a kitchen thermometer, and when the milk has reached the right temperature, remove it from the heat and stir in the dry milk.
2. Cool the milk until it registers between 105°F and 110°F on the thermometer, and stir in the plain yogurt. Pour the mixture into sterilized glass jars.
3. Incubate the yogurt for 4 to 8 hours by trying one of the following several methods. Depending on the method you use, you will have to check a few times during the incubation period to see if the yogurt mixture has reached the consistency of custard. When it has, the yogurt is ready to refrigerate. Yogurt will keep for 2 to 4 weeks in the refrigerator.

   To incubate yogurt, you can try one of the following

methods, all of which keep the culture at the proper 100°F temperature:

- Pour the yogurt into the containers that come with your commercial yogurt maker and follow the manufacturer's instructions.
- Place the jars and a thermometer in an insulated picnic cooler, cover carefully with a towel, and close the cooler. Check only once or twice, and add a jar of warm water if the temperature goes down.
- Place the jars, covered with a towel, in a 100°F oven.
- Alternatively, place the jars, covered, on a rack in an electric frying pan. Pour in an inch or two of warm water, set the thermostat on the pan to 100°F, and cover the pan.

TO USE Yogurt can be eaten plain, if you have acquired a taste for it, and it is delicious as a substitute for sour cream.

To flavor yogurt, simply add a teaspoon of honey or a tablespoon of your own Freezer Fruit Preserves (page 60). You can add ground cinnamon, Powdered Vanilla Sugar (page 180), and any other spices and flavors that suit your fancy. You can also make Frozen Fruiti Yogurt (page 61).

Makes 32 ounces yogurt

Homemade Cream Cheese

It's fun to make your own creamy, very creamy cheese. If your first attempts result in a cheese that is too thick or too thin, try adding some mushrooms or chili sauce to the cheese and serve it as a dip. You will need a kitchen thermometer for this recipe, as well as some cheesecloth.

> 1 gallon whole milk
> 1 quart cultured buttermilk
> ½ teaspoon salt

1. Pour the milk and buttermilk into a large pan and suspend the thermometer in the milk. Cook over medium heat, stirring occasionally, until the temperature registers 170°F.
2. Keep the mixture on the heat and keep the temperature of the milk between 170°F and 175°F. After 30 minutes, the mixture should start to separate into curds (the lumps) and whey (the liquid).
3. Line a strainer with several layers of moistened cheesecloth and set it inside a large bowl or pan to catch the drippings. Using a slotted spoon, lift the curds from the milk mixture and transfer them to the cheesecloth-lined strainer. Pour the remainder of the whey through the cheesecloth.
4. Let the curds drain, at room temperature, for 2 to 4 hours. Remove the cheese from the cheesecloth and place in blender with the salt. Blend until creamy.
5. Store the cheese in small, clean containers with tight-fitting lids and refrigerate. The cheese can also be frozen, thawed, and then beaten in a blender until creamy.

Makes 64 ounces cream cheese

Healthy Seed Treats

Here's a recipe that's not only healthy, but can also be a snack for our Halloween specials. It's homemade pumpkin seeds.

When you carve your Halloween pumpkin, save all the seeds you scoop out—they make delicious treats that are good for you as well as tasty.

> ½ cup salt
> 4 cups water
> 2 cups sunflower, pumpkin, melon, or squash
>   seeds, cleaned

1. In a large bowl, combine the salt and water and soak the seeds in the salted water for 12 hours.
2. Preheat the oven to 200°F. Oil a baking sheet.
3. Drain the seeds, dry with paper towels, and spread on the prepared pan in a single layer. Bake for 30 minutes, stirring the seeds often during the cooking time. Cool and store in an airtight container. The seeds will keep well for 4 to 6 weeks.

Makes 16 ounces healthy seeds

VARIATION   You can salt or season the seeds, depending on your tastes, with Sesame Seasoning Salt (page 197) or another combination of your favorite spices.

Healthy Bread Crumbs

These bread crumbs are healthy, both for your body and your wallet. If you use all the bread that comes your way, you will soon have a dandy mixture of whole wheat, rye, and various other interesting grains.

It's always a good idea to get into the habit of saving the ends and bits of breads to use in recipes and to give to the birds, especially in a snow-laden winter when birds provide the only color in the landscape outside your window.

2 cups stale bread

1. Preheat the oven to 250°F.
2. Arrange the bread in a single layer on a shallow baking sheet. Bake for 20 minutes to crisp. Set aside to cool.
3. Break the bread into small pieces and feed, slowly, into a blender or a food processor to make crumbs. Store the crumbs in an airtight container. The crumbs will keep for several weeks on the pantry shelf and indefinitely in the freezer. You can continue to replenish your supply as you collect stale bread. Stir the new bread crumbs into the old to combine.

Italiano Bread Crumbs

2 cups Healthy Bread Crumbs (above)
¼ cup grated Parmesan cheese
2 tablespoons dried parsley
2 sprigs fresh parsley, chopped
1 teaspoon dried oregano
1 teaspoon dried basil
1 teaspoon garlic powder

Combine all of the ingredients and store in an airtight container in the refrigerator for up to 2 months.

Sweet Crumbs

2 cups cookies, crackers, sweet buns, or dry cake
1 tablespoon brown sugar

Grind the ingredients in a blender for 1 minute, or until you have a fine-textured crumb. Store in an airtight container in the refrigerator or freezer for up to 2 months. To replenish your supply, stir any new crumbs thoroughly into the existing mixture.

Makes 20 ounces crumbs

Cheese Thins

Here's another old-timey flavor that was a treat when we were kids. Perfect for late-night listening, try also making up a batch of these for a football-watching party and serve them along with a bowl of Gazpacho-style Sauce (page 104), for dipping, or as an accompaniment to a hearty bowl of homemade soup.

>   1 cup all-purpose flour
>   1 teaspoon salt
>   ¼ teaspoon paprika
>   2 cups grated cheddar cheese
>   ½ cup (1 stick) butter

1. Sift the flour, salt, and paprika together in a large bowl and stir in the cheese.
2. Cream the butter in a food processor or using an electric mixer. Slowly add the flour mixture and mix until well blended.
3. Shape the mixture into a roll about three inches in diameter, and wrap the roll in wax paper. Chill in the refrigerator overnight.
4. Preheat the oven to 350°F. Grease a baking sheet.
5. Slice the chilled log very thinly. Roll and twist the slices into little crescents. Place on the prepared baking sheet.

Bake for 10 minutes, rotating the baking sheet, if necessary. Cool and store in a tightly closed container for 1 to 2 weeks.

Makes 24 ounces cheese thins

Herby Vegetable Crackers

I love crackers. I can sit in front of my computer, listen to the radio, or even watch television and munch away on flavored crackers. The problem is that store-bought crackers, though tasty enough, are full of preservatives to give them enough shelf life to last through geological epochs.

What's a cracker-lover to do? Make 'em yourself in advance so you can enjoy them any time. Here's how:

> 2 cups all-purpose flour
> 2 teaspoons mixed dried herbs: parsley, chives,
>   oregano, savory, thyme, tarragon
> ¼ cup dried celery (see page 162)
> ¼ cup dried onion (see page 162)
> ¼ cup sugar
> 1 teaspoon salt
> ½ teaspoon baking soda
> ¼ cup shortening
> 1 tablespoon oil
> ¾ cup warm water

1. In a large bowl, combine all of the ingredients, including shortening and oil, but not the water, stirring the dry ingredients together first to blend well. Slowly add the water and stir well.

2. Continue to stir until a smooth dough forms. Divide the dough in half, cover, and let it stand at room temperature for 10 minutes.

3. Preheat the oven to 400°F. Lightly oil a baking sheet.

4. Place half of the dough on the prepared baking sheet, flatten with a rolling pin, and roll the dough out to the edges of the pan. Use extra flour, if needed, on the pin to prevent the dough from sticking.

5. Cut the dough into 1-inch squares and prick them all over with the tines of a fork. Bake for 10 minutes until crisp but not brown. Transfer to wire racks to cool. Repeat with the remaining dough.

Makes 5 dozen crackers

Fat-Free Faux Corn

For those of us who are health conscious, even overly so, late-night popcorn feasts may make us feel guilty. So here's a recipe for something we call popcorn that can make it into any healthy lifestyle guide.

This is crunchy, satisfying, low in calories, and full of plant sterols for cholesterol control. In fact, given the balancing test between calories and sterols, this is a kind of superfood that will assuage hunger, appeal to the chewing reflex, and improve your health all at the same time.

> One 16-ounce package celery
> One 16-ounce package carrots
> 1 small yellow onion
> Chopped peanuts or cashews (optional)

¼ teaspoon Spicy Lemon Salt Substitute (page 196)

Tabasco or your favorite hot sauce (optional)

1. Mince the celery and add to a large bowl. Mince the carrots and combine with celery in the bowl. Peel and mince the onion and toss with celery and carrots.
2. Add the peanuts or cashews, if using, and toss. Sprinkle on the salt substitute. Season with Tabasco to taste, if desired. Refrigerate the mixture until well chilled.

Makes 36 ounces faux corn

Healthy Potato Chips

Make these in a big batch in advance, package them in small or large refrigerator bags, and they're ready to break out when *Coast* starts, or to slip into the kids' lunch bags.

Try all different kinds of seasonings to flavor your chips until you find the perfect mixture. I season mine up with sea salt and different types of vinegar, usually malt vinegar. You can make a Mexican-flavored chip by using ¼ cup of the Mexican Seasoning Mix (page 199) and dip the chips into a variety of dips: guacamole, sour cream, or refried beans.

2 pounds potatoes
¼ cup vegetable oil
¼ cup assorted seasonings: salt, onion salt, garlic powder, Firehouse Hot Chili Powder (page 200), grated Parmesan cheese

1. Preheat the oven to 450°F. Oil a large baking sheet.
2. Scrub the potatoes and slice as thinly as you possibly can, or slice using a food processor, fitted with the slicing attachment.
3. Spread the slices out in a single layer on the prepared baking sheet. Brush the tops of potatoes with oil. Bake for 8 to 10 minutes until the potatoes are golden brown, rotating the pan, if necessary.
4. While still warm, place the chips in a clean paper bag, add ¼ cup of the seasonings of your choice, and shake well.

Makes 2 pounds chips

Peach Chutney

If you like Indian food, especially if you like to spread a nicely seasoned chutney on naan or any other type of warm flatbread, you'll enjoy this recipe because this chutney perks up any meal or snack. It's a quick shot of taste late at night with some chai or regular black or green tea.

The recipe makes a nice batch of chutney that you can also use to accompany main courses, or to serve as a before-dinner palate teaser with some crackers or toasted wheat bread.

4 quarts peaches
5 cups white vinegar
½ cup chopped onions
½ cup sugar
½ cup raisins
¼ cup mustard seeds

2 ounces fresh ginger, peeled and minced, or
   1 teaspoon ground ginger
2 tablespoons crushed red pepper flakes
5 to 6 garlic cloves, chopped

1. Peel, pit, and quarter the peaches. Place the peaches in a saucepan and add 2 cups of the vinegar. Cook over medium heat for 30 minutes, or until the peaches are soft.
2. Add the remaining 3 cups vinegar and the onions, sugar, raisins, mustard seeds, ginger, red pepper, and garlic cloves. Cook for 15 minutes more.
3. Pour the chutney, while still hot, into sterilized canning jars and store in the refrigerator. The chutney will keep for 2 to 4 months.

Makes 48 ounces chutney

Presto Pesto

It's almost like magic how parsley and cilantro can help to clear your system of unwanted metals if you are thinking about doing a cleanse. And after listening to some of our shows, I think you will probably consider this version of the Italian staple.

This pesto mixture can be spread on fresh bread, pasta, or even rice for a stick-to-your-ribs meal.

  ½ cup sunflower seeds
  ½ cup pumpkin seeds
  ½ cup Brazil nuts, macadamia nuts, or the
     traditional pine nuts
  1 cup chopped fresh parsley

1 cup chopped fresh cilantro
1 cup cold-pressed, extra-virgin olive oil
3 garlic cloves
Pinch of sea salt
¼ cup fresh lemon juice

1. Soak the seeds and nuts in water overnight to release the enzyme inhibitors.
2. Process the parsley, cilantro, and olive oil in a blender until finely minced.
3. Add the garlic, nuts and seeds, salt, and lemon juice and process until the mixture is finely blended into a paste.
4. Store the pesto, topped with more olive oil, in a dark glass jar in the refrigerator. You can also freeze pesto for later use.

Makes about 1 cup pesto

Micro Veggies

Sometimes healthy snacks are so simple and so easy to make, it's scary. You ask yourself, if healthy food is this tasty, if it's so simple and quick to prepare, if it can resurrect vegetables that have been in the bottom of the bin for way too long, how come not everybody knows about this? Why isn't someone shouting this out or broadcasting it over the air?

That's exactly what I'm doing about micro veggies. At its most basic, this recipe is a very handy way to use up that celery, those scallions, the crooked carrots, or that large, now-shriveling, green bell pepper you bought with the best intentions a couple of weeks ago, didn't touch, and saw wither and dry on your refrigerator shelf.

Now these vegetables look ugly and dry, but you hate to

throw them out. As you look at the devastation on the shelf, relax. You can revitalize these, and in the process revitalize yourself, with a very healthy snack or even an appetizer for a meal. They also make for a good lunch box or brown bag snack.

The trick for turning these veggies into just such a snack is to dry them in your microwave oven. Dried veggies will keep on a pantry shelf far longer than you first thought they would keep in your refrigerator.

> 1 to 2 cups vegetables (celery, carrots, sweet
>   bell peppers, mushrooms, onions, and
>   scallions) all finely chopped and in any
>   proportion
> Salt and/or freshly ground black pepper or your
>   favorite spices

1. Cover a microwave tray with paper towels and spread the rinsed off and finely chopped vegetables out in a thin layer over the paper towels. Blot off any moisture from the vegetables with another paper towel; this will speed up the drying process.
2. Dry vegetables in your microwave on its low setting for 15 minutes. Rotate the tray during the cooking if your oven doesn't automatically rotate, and cook for another 15 minutes. After cooking for 30 minutes, check to make sure that the vegetables are dry to the touch.
3. Season to taste with salt and/or pepper or your favorite spices.
4. Allow the vegetables to cool and store in a container, as airtight as possible. Your vegetables will keep for 6 months on your pantry shelf.

TO USE   Eat these veggies as a crisp snack, use as a topping for a salad along with your croutons, or turn an everyday packet of beef or chicken bouillon into something quite delicious and surprising by adding them to your soup.

Makes 1 to 2 cups dried veggies

Turkey and Sprouts

It used to be you could only find bean sprouts in health food stores, but now you can find bean sprouts in just about any supermarket as well as any grocery or, in New York, any local Korean deli. Sprouts are healthy and add a nice contrasting taste to any sandwich, but especially a nice turkey sandwich.

You can prepare this sandwich in a variety of ways, hot or cold, grilled or pressed, or on ciabatta bread or panini bread or a multigrain or whole wheat. My favorite is a pita pocket. Here's my version of turkey and sprouts.

> 1 whole wheat pita roll
> 3 to 4 slices deli turkey, preferably honey,
>   smoked, or mesquite
> 2 to 3 slices tomato
> Vinaigrette dressing, preferably raspberry,
>   and/or hearty Polish mustard
> 1 handful fresh bean sprouts
> Fresh chopped parsley or cilantro

1. Stuff a pita pocket with turkey slices so that the entire inside is filled.
2. Add the tomato slices. Add the salad dressing and/or mustard. Stuff the pocket with bean sprouts, sprinkle on parsley or cilantro, and press together.

Makes 1 sandwich

VARIATION   You can toast the pita pocket first by splitting it and placing in toaster on "light." This adds more crispness to the sandwich.

Herbal Vinegar

And here's a nice herbal vinegar for your salad dressing.

¼ cup dried marjoram
¼ cup dried mint
2 tablespoons dried basil
2 tablespoons dried tarragon
1 tablespoon dried rosemary
½ teaspoon dried dill
½ teaspoon dried allspice
½ teaspoon ground cloves
1 quart apple cider vinegar

1. Place all of the ingredients in a sterilized glass jar or crock, cover, and let stand in a cool, dry place for 4 weeks. Stir and mash the herbs once a day.
2. Strain the vinegar through a cheesecloth-lined strainer or a coffee filter. Pour the clear vinegar into sterilized glass jars or bottles, cap or cork, and store in the pantry for up to 4 months.

Makes 32 ounces vinegar

VARIATIONS   Other herbs to try include summer savory or thyme; 1 cup white wine may be added to the vinegar, and as an added touch, it's always pretty to return a stalk or two of a fresh herb to the clear, bottled vinegar.

Mix Herbal Vinegar with 2 tablespoons of Great Seasonings

Salad Dressing Mix (page 198) for a tasty salad dressing.

Even more intriguing on warm summer nights is this variation for Mint Vinegar. Place 2 cups fresh mint leaves and 1 quart white or apple cider vinegar in a sterilized glass jar, cover, and store in a cool, dry place for 2 weeks. Crush and stir the mixture every day. Strain and store as for other vinegars. Try freezing mint vinegar into cubes in an ice cube tray and add to lemonade and other summer drinks.

Raspberry Vinegar

Let's say you want a healthy salad to perk you up in the evening. Nothing too heavy because you have to get up early in the morning, but don't want to miss tonight's guest. So a salad, maybe with a little lemon juice sprinkled on top with a great light dressing is just the thing. Try this for starters over some romaine lettuce, fresh parsley, and some cut-up fresh basil leaves.

The basic recipe for vinegar with raspberries can be varied to take advantage of other fruits and herbs you might have in abundance.

1 pound fresh raspberries
3 cups malt vinegar
3 cups sugar

1. Rinse the raspberries gently and place them in a sterilized glass jar. Stir in the vinegar and mash the berries a bit with a spoon. Cover and store in a cool, dry place for 3 days.
2. Strain the vinegar from the berries through a cheesecloth-lined strainer or a coffee filter and discard the fruit pulp.

3. Place the vinegar in a nonreactive pan, add the sugar, and bring to a boil. Boil for 5 minutes, stirring constantly, until the sugar has dissolved. Set aside to cool.

4. Pour the vinegar into sterilized bottles or jars and cover or cork tightly. The vinegar will keep in the pantry for up to 4 months.

TO USE   Try a cooling, snappy summer drink. Mix ½ cup Raspberry Vinegar with 1 cup water, pour over ice, add lemon and mint, and serve.

Try mixing the fruit vinegar with mild olive oil, salt, and pepper and drizzle over fresh fruit and avocado wedges for a tangy summer salad.

Makes 3 cups vinegar

VARIATION   Use other berries in this recipe for different flavors and combinations. Try blueberries mixed with ½ cup chopped lemon or strawberries and oranges.

Apple Congee

This is an old German remedy for intestinal distress that I learned about from some neighbors. Give it a try before you move on to more serious remedies.

What is a congee? It is rice, your favorite kind of rice from Texas long rice to basmati, to yellow rice, to brown rice, or even to risotto cooked with double the amount of water so it becomes more of a soup dish. Eat it by the spoonful when it's nice and hot, and it will settle you down for the night and ease any intestinal discomfort.

3 cups water
2 cups rice
1 cup unsweetened apple juice
2 tart apples, peeled, cored, and sliced
Ground cinnamon, to taste

1. Pour the water into a saucepan, add the rice, and bring to a boil. Immediately reduce to a simmer and add the apple juice.
2. In a separate saucepan, cook apples in just enough water to cover them until they are soft.
3. Add the cooked apples to the warm rice.
4. Cover and cook for another 10 minutes at a low simmer.
5. Remove from the heat and dust with ground cinnamon.

Makes 2 cups congee

Freezer Fruit Preserves

When you freeze your fruit jams and preserves, you make the most healthy choice for yourself and your family. You also save yourself all the trouble of hot-water canning, coating with paraffin, and making sure the seals are secure. If you have a lot of freezer space, you can enjoy a very fresh-tasting preserve.

4 cups strawberries
8 cups sugar
1½ cups water
2 tablespoons powdered fruit pectin
2 tablespoons fresh lemon juice

1. Clean the berries, place in a large bowl, and crush them a bit. Add the sugar and stir gently to mix. Set the bowl aside and let the berries macerate for 10 minutes.
2. In a saucepan, combine the water and pectin and bring to a boil. Boil for 1 minute, stirring constantly.
3. Pour the water-pectin mixture over the strawberries and stir to mix and to mash the berries a bit more. Stir in the lemon juice.
4. Pour the fruit into freezer containers or sterilized glass jars, leaving room for expansion. Cover and let sit at room temperature overnight.
5. On the next day, refrigerate one jar for immediate use, if desired, and freeze the other containers. The preserves will keep for up to 9 months in the freezer.

Makes 10 cups preserves

VARIATIONS   Many other fruits can be made into quick freezer preserves. For example, try freezing freshly crushed blueberries, raspberries, or cranberries and chopped lemon.

Frozen Fruit Yogurt

If you are making up a nice batch of creamy Homemade Yogurt, you will undoubtedly have enough on hand to turn into frozen fruit-flavored yogurt pops.

> 2 cups plain Homemade Yogurt (page 42)
> 1 cup fresh or frozen fruit: banana, orange,
>   strawberries, raspberries, or a combination
> ¼ cup honey

1. Puree the yogurt and fruit in a blender, and add the honey once the fruit is well blended.
2. Pour the mixture into a freezer container: an ice cube tray, a shallow plastic container, or a 9-inch-square cake pan. Freeze for 30 minutes.
3. Spoon the frozen mush into the blender container and blend for 1 minute. Pour the mixture into Popsicle molds or paper cups. Freeze for 10 minutes, insert Popsicle sticks, and return to freezer until firm.

Makes 20 ounces frozen yogurt

VARIATIONS   Spices and other flavorings can be added as you experiment with fruit and yogurt combinations. For example, try ½ teaspoon vanilla, ½ teaspoon ground cinnamon, and ½ teaspoon ground nutmeg whipped up with 1 banana.

Or, try mixing 6 ounces frozen juice concentrate with 1 cup yogurt and 1 teaspoon vanilla.

Unadulterated Adult Herbal Teas

Try making some of your very own seasoned and herbal teas, and if you find a blend that particularly suits you, remember that it would make a nice gift for someone else to sample. A word of caution: never try to brew a tea from an herb you can't identify. Even though a certain herb may look small and harmless, it could be dangerous and even lethal.

You can buy all the herbs listed in the following blends at the health food store or through a mail-order firm on the Internet. Or, if you are patient, you can plan ahead and begin to grow some of the herbs in your annual or perennial flower beds.

Good Digestion Tea

  2 tablespoons dried peppermint leaves
  1 tablespoon dried rosemary
  1 tablespoon dried comfrey leaves

1. Blend the herbs and store in an airtight container.
2. To make the tea, steep 1 tablespoon of the tea mix in 1 cup of water for 5 minutes.

Balmy Lemon Tea

  9 tablespoons dried lemon thyme
  3 tablespoons dried lemon basil
  2 tablespoons dried chamomile
  1 tablespoon dried lemon balm

1. Blend the herbs and store in an airtight container.
2. To make tea, steep as above. Lemon balm is said to reduce fevers, so you might sip this tea if you feel a fever coming on.

Makes 2 ounces tea mix

VARIATIONS   The following herbs will make a nice tea, alone or in combination. Test and find the flavors you like best.

  • Anise will give you a sweet licorice flavor that is supposed to be good for coughs and an aid to sleep.
  • Chamomile is mild, apple flavored, very soothing, and is said to prevent nightmares.
  • Catnip has a very strong flavor and is said to have been an old-fashioned cough remedy. It is probably best to leave it to your cats.

• Dill and fennel are familiar and strongly flavored. Boil the seeds for tea.

• Lavender imparts a delicate and unusual fragrance and flavor when mixed with other herbs in tea.

• Rose hips are an excellent source of vitamin C and add a fruity, spicy flavor.

• Rosemary and sage, both kitchen favorites, are spicy and soothing to sore throats.

• Strawberry leaves and fruit make a sweet and fragrant tea.

3

· ANCIENT WORLD ·

Hurried Curried Pockets

Chicken or Turkey Fried Rice

Quick Turkey or Chicken Enchiladas

Stir-Fried Turkey or Chicken with Broccoli or Peppers

East India Chutney

Auntie's Turkey Salad

Turkey or Chicken Caesar Salad

Chicken or Turkey Couscous

Turkey or Chicken Asian Fusion Salad

Pully Slabs of Bread

Asian Congee

Quick Turkey Potpie

Turkey and Guacamole

English Toffee

Tortoni

Honey Gelato

Many of our food choices in the modern kitchen come from our long-forgotten past. The ancient world, as we discuss at least once a week, is not fully known or properly taught. New discoveries about our earliest ancestors are taking place all the time, rewriting the history of human civilization and even pointing to possible outside—read "otherworldly"—influences in our development.

While some of us were painting on cave walls, some of us were stirring the pot—making stews from meat at hand and treacly treats to cover the sour taste of strange fruit.

Hurried Curried Pockets

No matter where you hail from, East or West, North or South, the taste of curry can add an exotic flavor to any chicken, beef, or lamb stew, or even straight on vegetables. Another exotic treat for me is to prepare my own curry seasoning to keep on hand and sprinkle on a pita bread, microwave the bread, and enjoy it straight up or spread with my own yogurt or Greek yogurt from the market. It's a snack that, once you've made your curry seasoning, takes only minutes to cook up and is a burst of flavor at night.

First, here is an easy recipe for a very authentic curry powder you can use to flavor a pita or any other flatbread, especially naan. This is much fresher than the dried powder that has been on your grocer's shelf for weeks or even months. And since this is so fresh, you can prepare it in small portions for your pita or naan.

CURRY POWDER
1 tablespoon cumin seeds
1 tablespoon cardamom seeds
1 tablespoon coriander seeds
2 tablespoons ground turmeric
1 tablespoon dry mustard
½ teaspoon cayenne pepper

Pita or naan bread

1. Combine the cumin, cardamom, and coriander seeds in a microwave-safe glass or enamel container, and cover and shake to make sure they are blended.
2. Microwave on low for 6 minutes, rotate, and microwave on

low for another 5 minutes. Let stand in the microwave for another 2 minutes to cool and for the flavors to meld so as to even out.

3. Grind the microwaved seeds in your blender at high speed and then add the turmeric, mustard, and cayenne. Mix again for a minute or two to make sure that all of the spices are completely blended.

4. Use immediately or store in a tightly capped container. The curry powder will keep for a year or more in your pantry if sealed properly.

5. To make your curried pockets, sprinkle curry powder on your bread. Heat the flatbread in your microwave for 15 seconds and you have a restaurant-level treat.

Makes 3 ounces curry powder; as many pockets as you wish

VARIATIONS   Add the curry powder to any stew, chicken, beef, lamb, or even straight on vegetables for an exotic flavor. This is also an especially good spice for any lentil bean soup.

Curried mayonnaise makes an interesting sandwich spread. Add a bit of your homemade curry powder to your favorite brand of mayonnaise or your own homemade mayonnaise recipe and use it for turkey, turkey club, chicken, or BLT sandwiches.

Croutons, too, can be spiced up with your homemade curry mix. At the final stage of tossing your homemade croutons, or just using store-bought plain croutons, sprinkle with homemade curry powder, toss, and either pop these croutons as a snack anytime, especially as a late-night treat, or use the curried croutons on your simple salads or soups.

Chicken or Turkey Fried Rice

It's surprising how easy it is to make fried rice. I make it all the time, not only from scratch, but from leftover rice from a Chinese takeout. In fact, in LA, where there is a fast-food Chinese restaurant on just about every corner from the Marina to downtown LA and from Hollywood all the way to Woodland Hills, you can pick up a container of rice on your way home and use it as the rice for your own fried rice.

I can hear the skeptics out there saying, "If you're buying the rice from the restaurant, why are you making your own fried rice?" Because my own fried rice is fresher, I can vary the flavors, use up what I have on hand, and I can make my own version of my favorite fried rice dish that I frequently eat at Mao's Kitchen in beautiful downtown Venice, California.

I love fried rice, not just because it's easy to make and tasty, but you can vary the flavor in many different ways. So, it's versatile. I'll make up a batch for lunch, or for a side dish at dinner, and sometimes just have it for a snack late at night.

Just like the recipe for Stir-Fried Turkey or Chicken with Broccoli or Peppers (page 73), you'll need a wok or a deep wok-shaped sauté or chef's pan and a wooden spatula or long chopsticks. You want to use wood, not metal or rubberized plastic.

> 2 cups or more of rice you've prepared from
>   scratch or leftover rice
> 1 to 2 cups minced, cooked turkey or chicken
>   (You can also use sliced cooked beef, of
>   course, or you can combine your poultry and
>   beef for a "house special.")
> 1 medium onion, finely sliced
> 6 shallots, diced

1 large egg
1 tablespoon peanut oil
Soy sauce
1 teaspoon hot chili oil
Hot sauce

1. Cut or slice your meat, onions, and shallots into very thin slices and set aside. I can't emphasize enough that the slices have to be very thin, especially the sliced meat, because the trick of stir-fry wok cooking is that these small, thin slices will fry quickly over high heat. So make those slices *very thin*.
2. Beat the egg in a small bowl and set aside.
3. Heat half of the peanut oil over high heat and then add the meat (turkey, chicken, or beef), stirring rapidly as the meat browns. When the meat is brown, remove it from the wok and set aside. You can also taste one of the thin slices of meat for doneness because you want the meat to be thoroughly cooked.
4. Add the remaining peanut oil to the hot wok, add rice, and stir-fry quickly, browning the rice.
5. Add the onions and shallots and stir quickly through the rice. Stir-fry for a couple of minutes to allow the flavors to blend. Return the meat to the wok and continue to stir-fry. Add a splash or two of soy sauce as you stir-fry.
6. Form a hollow ring at the center of the fried rice in the wok and pour the egg into the center of the ring while stirring the egg rapidly. Work the fried egg through the entire fried rice mixture, then add the chili oil, hot sauce, and more soy sauce to taste. Remove from the heat and serve.

Makes 4 to 5 servings depending on whether this is a main dish or a side dish

VARIATION   Whether or not you are preparing your fried rice with meat or keeping it simply vegetarian, here's a variation that I love. In addition to frying the egg in the center of the fried rice mixture, in a separate frying pan fry another egg, omelet style, and when cooked, slide the omelet over the top of the fried rice and then add more hot sauce and soy sauce. It's a meal in itself and absolutely delicious.

Quick Turkey or Chicken Enchiladas

This is a baked casserole dish that you can prepare in advance of your late-night radio listening, keep in the refrigerator, and reheat in sections, just like a lasagna, in your regular oven, toaster oven, or microwave.

An enchilada casserole can be as spicy or as mild as you like, but it is basically a combination of meat, chili peppers and onions, sour cream as a topping, cheese, and tortilla strips laid out on top. You can also wrap your enchilada casserole in whole tortillas for an enchilada wrap with some great hot sauce.

And for still another variation for your cookout, prepare the enchilada casserole in advance, then reheat on aluminum foil over an open charcoal or wood fire, heat the tortillas over the fire very gently, wrap your enchiladas, and have a feast.

If you've ever watched how lasagna is built—meat and sausage and peppers and onions on the bottom of the baking dish, then long lasagna noodles, sauce, then cheese, then additional layers of meat, noodles, sauce, and cheese—you'll understand how to prepare your enchiladas. Accordingly, you will need one medium, deep baking dish for each batch of enchilada casserole.

1 pound cooked turkey or chicken either cubed
    or cut into long, moderately thin slices (see
    Note)
1 teaspoon olive or vegetable oil
One 8-ounce can chicken bouillon
1 cup or an 8-ounce container sour cream
One 8-ounce can cream of chicken soup or
    turkey gravy, thinned out with ¼ cup water
1 cup minced green chile peppers or mild
    jalapeños
One 16-ounce package corn or wheat tortillas
½ cup shredded Monterey or Colby-Jack cheese
½ cup shredded cheddar cheese or prepackaged
    Mexican cheese mixture

1. Preheat the oven to 375°F. Coat the bottom of a heatproof dish with oil and set on the stovetop to warm on the lowest setting.

2. Combine the sour cream, soup or thinned out gravy, and chile peppers.

3. Spread one layer of the soup-chile-cream mixture over the bottom of the baking dish.

4. Cut each individual tortilla into strips. Cover soup-chile-cream layer with long tortilla strips. Next cover that layer with turkey or chicken. Add additional layers until you reach near, but not at, the top because this casserole will bubble over as it cooks.

5. Cover the top of the casserole with the shredded cheese mixture.

6. Cover the baking dish with aluminum foil and bake for 45 minutes.

7. Remove the foil and bake for another 5 to 10 minutes to crisp the cheese slightly.

Makes 6 to 8 servings depending on the serving size

NOTE   This recipe assumes you have leftover turkey or chicken from the day before. However, if you are roasting the turkey or chicken, then you should cook it in a preheated oven at 350°F, or no lower than 325°F, until the internal temperature reaches 185°F. You can use a meat thermometer to check the internal temperature. Cook a 3-pound bird at 325° to 350°F for 2 hours. Larger birds, say 5 to 6 pounds, should cook for 3 hours, but check the internal temperature. Experienced cooks also test for doneness by wiggling the turkey or chicken leg. If it seems to come off the body easily, the bird is done.

Green chile peppers are a staple of New Mexico–style cooking, and you can enjoy all kinds of green chile dishes when you visit Roswell for their anniversary celebrations every year.

VARIATION   You can turn this casserole into an enchilada wrap by spooning the mixture onto hot tortillas, wrapping them, and placing them back in the oven for 5 minutes or on an open fire until they become crisp. For softer tortillas, wrap them in foil over an open fire.

Stir-Fried Turkey or Chicken with Broccoli or Peppers

The best pot to use for making anything stir-fried is either a wok or a wok-shaped sauté or chef's pan for cooking in smaller batches. Woks, at least the ones accomplished chefs use, are seasoned so that the food doesn't stick.

Seasoning the pan is not hard, but it takes repeated use. The standard seasoning instruction involves your heating peanut oil, which you'll use for your stir-frying in any event, on high heat in the wok, and then draining the oil and wiping the cooling wok down with a towel.

After a few times, your new wok will be nice and seasoned and ready for your stir-frying. Remember, woks don't go into the dishwasher. Just wipe clean and let dry.

> 1 cup, or more for larger servings, leftover cooked turkey or chicken, thinly sliced or finely chopped
>
> 1 medium bell pepper, seeded and very thinly sliced
>
> 1 medium onion, very thinly sliced
>
> One 16-ounce package frozen broccoli
>
> 1 teaspoon peanut oil
>
> 1 garlic clove (optional)
>
> One 8-ounce can sliced Chinese water chestnuts, drained
>
> 1 teaspoon hot chili oil
>
> Tabasco or your favorite hot sauce
>
> Soy sauce

1. Prepare the bell peppers and onions first and set aside on the countertop, a large plate, or a cutting board. Once the stir-frying starts, you will have no time for cutting or slicing.
2. If you are using frozen broccoli, cook in a separate saucepan, following the package directions.
3. Heat the peanut oil and garlic, if using, in a wok over very high heat. Add the vegetables, stirring rapidly to coat with the oil. Stir with a wooden spatula or chopsticks. Don't use metal or plastic utensils. Metal will scratch the surface of the wok and plastic will melt.

4. Add the turkey or chicken, and stir-fry carefully but rapidly. Add the water chestnuts and continue to stir-fry. Add the chili oil and Tabasco to taste. Sprinkle with soy sauce to taste and stir through so that all of the ingredients are coated. Remove from the heat.

5. This entire dish should take no more than 10 or so minutes to make and serve. Serve over rice, serve rice on the side, or even wrap in a heated wheat tortilla. For a fun variation, if you are serving this rice, make your own fried rice (see page 69), which you can also make as a separate dish with turkey and chicken as well as beef.

Makes 4 servings

East India Chutney

This chutney keeps forever in the fridge, and can add a bit of distinction to an otherwise bland meal or snack. Indulge in the exotic!

12 apples, cored and chopped
4 cups firmly packed brown sugar
8 cups apple cider
4 cups raisins
1 onion, chopped
2 red bell peppers, seeded and chopped
¼ cup dry mustard
¼ cup ground ginger
1 tablespoon salt

1. Add all of the ingredients to a large bowl and mix to combine. Transfer the mixture to a large saucepan and bring to

a boil. Boil for 1 minute, reduce the heat to a simmer, and cook for 1 hour.

2. While still hot, pour the chutney into sterilized canning jars and store in the refrigerator. The chutney will keep for 2 to 4 months refrigerated.

Makes 48 ounces chutney

Auntie's Turkey Salad

Turkey is the easiest sandwich meat. Turkey is easy. You can stock up on it from your local market in a variety of tastes—honey-roasted, smoked, and just plain sliced. Put it in your fridge's meat keeper, make sure you have your favorite bread in your bread drawer, and you can put together a sandwich, from simple to complicated, in minutes.

Like garlic? There's plenty of sliced garlic bread to be had at most markets that is a perfect foil to smoked or honey-roasted turkey. Nice pumpernickel or pumpernickel and rye swirl bread offsets mesquite turkey nicely as well. Here are some sandwich ideas to play with, and some ingredients to add to your shopping list to make your own monster sandwich or light snack sandwich late at night during our news breaks on *Coast*.

The wonderful thing about turkey—and, remember, you can always replace turkey with white meat chicken—is that it's the kind of sandwich meat you can take anywhere and serve for any reason at any meal, especially brunch on the weekends. You can never go wrong with turkey.

Here is the turkey salad recipe my aunt used to make. She used an ice cream scoop to fill the hollowed-out tomatoes, peppers, or even avocados, but you can use a large serving spoon instead.

2 cups cubed cooked turkey or white meat chicken

4 to 5 celery stalks, minced

1 small onion, finely chopped or minced

1 small sweet green bell pepper, seeded and very
finely chopped or minced

¼ cup mayonnaise or Mustard Mayonnaise
(page 284)

1 tablespoon sweet pickle relish or India relish

3 to 4 medium, fresh ripe tomatoes

1. In a large bowl, mix together the turkey, celery, onion, and bell pepper until combined.
2. Add the plain or flavored mayonnaise and stir through until all of the ingredients are coated.
3. Add the pickle or India sweet relish and stir through. Taste and add more if desired.
4. Core and hollow out the tomatoes, and add the tomato pulp to your salad.
5. Spoon the salad into the hollowed out tomatoes and serve.

Makes 3 to 4 cups salad

VARIATIONS   Yes, Virginia, there are variations on this recipe depending on whether you want a nice, soft tomato surprise, a crunchy pepper surprise (be sure all of the seeds have been rinsed away or you'll be in for quite a real surprise), or a sweet and smooth avocado. Simply cut open the pepper at the top and rinse thoroughly to make sure all the tough membranes and seeds have been removed, and fill with the salad. If using an avocado, split it in two, reserve the pit for later planting, and spoon the salad into both halves.

This dish, fun late at night and very refreshing, reminds me of my aunty's house at the beach, salty air, and my uncle who'd come back from breakwater with a fresh catch of fish for dinner.

Turkey or Chicken Caesar Salad

Let's start out with some historical debunking. No, the Caesar salad was not named in honor of Julius or Augustus Caesar because, basically, they didn't invent the dish. Nor was the salad invented in Italy. Caesar salad was invented in Mexico, actually in Tijuana, back in the 1920s by a celebrated Italian chef named Caesar Cardini. In fact, some specialty grocery stores and Italian gourmet food stores may even have bottled Caesar Cardini dressings.

What is a Caesar salad? If you've enjoyed the show of having your Caesar salad prepared table side in a fancy schmancy restaurant, you know how your preparer whisks in a raw egg, anchovies, and the spices. By the way, anchovies—and there are two types of people in this world, those that love 'em and those that don't—were not in the original recipe. They were added later.

I happen to like anchovies and, when I build my salad, I lay the little guys right on top. But don't feel like an outcast if you make your salad without anchovies or anchovy paste. They are historically inaccurate to begin with.

Caesar salad does rely on a certain level of crunchiness, which comes from toasted bread squares or croutons. You can make them yourself without too much trouble, or you can do what I do and buy the packaged croutons, either Italian style or Caesar croutons. I recommend the Caesar croutons because you can also eat them right up out of the package as a snack. When using them in salad, I soak them in olive oil, or olive oil infused with garlic, first. (The infused oil is simple to make in advance. Just buy any good extra-virgin olive oil from the supermarket, peel and then crush 1 to 2 garlic cloves, and drop them into the olive oil where they slowly impart their flavor over time.)

As long as you're doing any infusing to make your own flavored olive oil, you can also try making your own hot Italian pepper. Dry it either slowly by hanging it on a thread over your counter or in your electric oven, and then chop it up very finely, and drop it into your extra-virgin olive oil. Trust me, infused olive oil is a very special treat.

Making the salad itself, if you are not making your own dressing, which is a form of art, is not hard. I recommend, however, that if you are getting your Caesar dressing from your supermarket, you get regular, not creamy, Caesar, and that you use Caesar-flavored croutons. After that, preparing your salad is quick and easy.

½ cup bottled Caesar dressing, regular or
   creamy, your choice
1 garlic clove, peeled and crushed
1 teaspoon lemon juice, either store-bought like
   ReaLemon, or just a squeeze of fresh lemon
1 tablespoon hearty mustard
¼ cup bottled capers, drained
1 head fresh romaine lettuce thoroughly washed
   and patted dry
1 medium red or yellow onion, minced
½ cup grated or shaved Parmesan or Pecorino
   Romano cheese
1 cup sliced or cubed leftover cooked turkey or
   chicken
1 cup, or more to taste, Caesar-flavored croutons
½ tin anchovies in oil (about 6 anchovies), for
   anchovy lovers only

1. In a small mixing bowl, combine the Caesar dressing with the crushed garlic, lemon juice, mustard, and half of the capers. Set aside to allow the flavors to meld.

2. In a large salad bowl, mix the lettuce with the onion and the remaining capers. Sprinkle on half of the cheese and toss.

3. Toss through the turkey or chicken. Add the croutons and toss (if you want crunchier croutons, add them after you've poured on the dressing and either toss or not).

4. Now add the salad dressing and top with the anchovies and the remaining cheese.

Makes 2 main-dish servings or 4 to 6 side salads depending on the size of the helping

VARIATION   If you want to get wacky about turning this turkey or chicken Caesar into a main dish for lunch or dinner, or even for a very, very late *Coast to Coast* dinner, you can also toss some peppered smoked salmon into the salad before you add the dressing for a very exotic taste.

Chicken or Turkey Couscous

I'm of Middle Eastern descent, and one of the famous dishes from the Middle East and northern Africa is something called couscous. Couscous is semolina wheat that has been shaped into coarse, tiny grain-like bits. When I'm making a couscous dinner, I do it the easy way, which I recommend to you, by getting instant or quick-cooking packaged couscous from the supermarket and then zapping it up with my own ingredients.

Simply follow the package directions by boiling the water, adding the couscous straight from the box, adding just a teaspoon of olive oil, a pinch of dried parsley, and some salt and crushed red pepper flakes, and then covering the saucepan and removing it from the heat. In ten minutes I have a very satisfying meal. But I don't stop there.

If I have leftover turkey or chicken, especially chicken that I have cooked on the grill with barbecue sauce, I like to serve it over the couscous, as a topping, or add it to the couscous after I've removed the saucepan from the heat and stir it through. Different days, different ways.

> One 10-ounce package plain couscous
> 1 chicken bouillon cube
> 4 to 5 green shallots, minced
> Pinch of dried parsley
> ½ to 1 cup cooked, cubed turkey or chicken
> Salt and freshly ground black pepper
> Tabasco or your favorite hot sauce (optional)

1. In a large saucepan, cook the couscous according to the package directions. (These usually ask that you bring a cup or two of water to a boil, and add a teaspoon or half teaspoon of olive oil.) When the water is boiling, add the bouillon cube, stir, remove the pan from the heat, add the couscous, and stir.

2. Add the shallots, parsley, and turkey or chicken, and immediately cover tightly. Let sit for 10 minutes until the couscous absorbs all of the water.

3. Season with salt and pepper to taste, add hot sauce, if that is what you like, and your ten-minute meal is complete.

Makes at least 2 servings, but can be stretched to 4

VARIATIONS   There are scores of variations of couscous dishes, all the way from pure vegan to beef couscous and even to adding cooked codfish or flaked cooked salmon. Couscous is one of the easiest dishes to prepare and is a great alternative to rice, pasta, or potatoes.

Adding chicken, turkey, beef, or fish enhances the couscous.

But even all by itself or with spices ranging from ground cumin to curry powder, couscous is fun to experiment with. You can even have piping hot couscous with a little cream for breakfast, as an alternative to regular hot or cold cereal. On a cold morning, instead of boiling water for instant oatmeal, cream of wheat, or grits, try boiling water and making a couscous breakfast, topped with raisins and cinnamon, and see if that doesn't do the trick.

A NOTE ABOUT BEEF   Certainly, you can replace most of the leftover turkey and chicken recipes with beef. I focused on the poultry because most folks, including myself, always seem to wind up with lots more poultry leftovers than anything else, especially during the holiday season.

I have seen turkeys in friends' refrigerators that have been stripped to the bone over a period of days as post-Thanksgiving family members consumed sandwich after sandwich, turkey pies, and turkey salads. Turkey, and to a lesser extent, chicken, is the meal that keeps on giving, and not just after Thanksgiving.

I have no prejudice against beef, I want you to know, and will enjoy a full-on hamburger whenever I want. Living part time in Southern California, the home of many an exotic hamburger fast-food chain, I have no compunctions about availing myself of the different varieties of hamburger from the Hamburger Hamlet in Century City around the corner from CAA, to our local Jerry's Famous Deli on Ventura in the Valley, to the unbelievable In/Out Burger stands dropped like hotels on a Monopoly board throughout Los Angeles.

So if you ask me, "Where's the beef?" I say, it's right here. Just replace the turkey with beef, especially in the stews, chili, and pot pie (making sure to flour the beef for stews and pot-pie), and you can say, "Here's the beef."

Turkey or Chicken Asian Fusion Salad

Assembling and tossing up this salad on a Sunday night when I'm listening to George Knapp on his *Coast to Coast* show is particularly enjoyable. Asian chicken or turkey salad is nice and tangy, spicy to taste, and always refreshing. You can add as much or as little cooked poultry as you like. The secret is in the fruit, some crunchy water chestnuts, and the tangy ginger dressing.

> 1 small head romaine or buttercup lettuce, washed and dried
> 1 cup or more sliced cooked turkey or chicken
> One 6-ounce can sliced Chinese water chestnuts, drained
> 1 cup canned Chinese Mandarin orange slices, or 1 small fresh tangerine, peeled and thinly sliced
> ¼ cup fresh California almonds
> ¼ cup shredded unsweetened coconut
> ½ cup of your favorite store-bought ginger salad dressing (see Note)
> 1 handful raisins, golden or dark (optional)

1. Wash and dry your lettuce leaves and place in a medium to large salad bowl, depending on how much salad you're making.
2. Add the chicken or turkey and toss.
3. Add the water chestnuts and the Mandarin orange slices or tangerine slices. Toss the salad to distribute all of the ingredients and then add the almonds and coconut and toss again.

4. Pour on the ginger dressing and, if you like, top with the raisins.

Makes an easy salad for 4 and can be stretched to 6

NOTE There are many brands of store-bought dressings to choose from when you need one. My favorites are the ones that require refrigeration because I've found firsthand through late-night salad-making on the fly that they're much more tangy.

Pully Slabs of Bread

Think about those soft bread sticks in a restaurant, just-baked and still hot as they're brought to your table. Think about that bagel shop in the mall where you can get bread twists and soft rolls that simply fall apart in your mouth.

You love 'em, I love 'em, and your kids love 'em. Now you can have them when you want them most, late at night, getting involved with what one of my guests has to say, and thinking that if you could only be noshing on something everything would be just about perfect.

This recipe for soft, savory slabs of bread is also very efficient because you can make up a large batch to reheat and serve as a snack, with a meal, or as a late-night treat even while the commercials are playing. Keep listening to the commercials, of course, because these are my sponsors, but you can make the soft savory bread while you do so.

> 1 large Italian loaf or French bread
> ½ cup (1 stick) butter, softened
> 2 tablespoons garlic powder

> 1½ teaspoons chili powder (optional, for a
>   Southwestern flavor)
> 1½ teaspoons ground cumin (optional, for a
>   Southwestern flavor)

1. Slice the bread crosswise, not lengthwise, making deep parallel cuts. However, don't cut through the bottom crust.
2. Coat the bread with the softened butter by brushing the butter along the top crust and the bottom crust.
3. Sprinkle on the seasonings of your choice, the garlic powder and ground chili powder and ground cumin, if using.
4. Put the bread back together, squeezing closed all the cuts, and wrap the entire loaf in an absorbent paper towel.
5. Microwave on high for 3 minutes, rotate, reduce the power to low, and microwave for 90 seconds more. If your microwave cannot adjust power, then microwave for 30 seconds on high.
6. Remove from the oven and while still hot, unwrap and cut bread sticks into 1- by 4-inch rectangles. Serve it, or just feast on it yourself.

Makes 4 servings, but only if you're generous

Asian Congee

A congee, as described in the Apple Congee recipe (page 59), is a basic Japanese staple dish that can be served at any mealtime during the day, from breakfast to a late-night snack. I became aware of this dish thanks to some of my Japanese friends, who told me that their parents would prepare congee for them when they were feeling sick or had any stomach discomfort.

It's basically a soupy rice dish that can be served in hundreds of different varieties, with meat, purely vegetarian, or just plain. There are also both Italian and German variations of this dish, served by parents to their children for hundreds of years.

My friend's German grandmother prepared this dish with apples (see page 59). My other friend's Italian grandmother prepared this dish with hot—and I mean really hot—peppers whenever he had a bad stomach upset. Cayenne, you should know, kills bad bacteria.

Here's the surprise: Asian families like to add a whole host of ingredients to this dish. Turkey congee, believe it or not, is an Asian variation of a leftover American Thanksgiving turkey dish.

> 4 cups water
> 1 cup favorite rice (If you are cooking risotto,
>   you have to increase the amount of liquid in
>   this recipe by another half.)
> Salt and pepper to taste

1. Bring the water and salt to a rolling boil in a medium to large saucepan. Don't stint on the salt because salt does have digestive benefits.
2. Add the rice, stirring as you add. Bring to a boil, stir, reduce the heat to a simmer, and cover. Check rice every 20 minutes for softness.
3. When the rice is cooked, season with your favorite sauce or just eat the soupy rice straight.

Makes 2 cups congee

VARIATIONS

◆ **Spicy Congee:** Add chopped hot jalapeño peppers or Tabasco sauce to the boiling water. Add the rice and continue to cook as above. Congee can be as spicy as you want.

◆ **Turkey or Chicken Congee:** Add ½ cup shredded, cooked turkey or chicken to the congee after the rice has become soft. Reduce the heat to a simmer and cook for another 10 minutes, or remove from the heat and microwave for 5 minutes. If you want a more intense taste, instead of the 4 cups of water, add 3 cups water and 1 cup chicken bouillon.

Quick Turkey Potpie

You don't have to be a senior citizen to slip a turkey potpie into the oven and enjoy the magic of the blend of flavors. I like potpies so much, especially using my Thanksgiving leftover birdie, that I came up with a very simple store-bought ingredients recipe for putting together a turkey potpie in about 30 minutes, the amount of time it would take you to heat up a store-bought frozen potpie.

By the way, you can replace the leftover turkey with chicken or even some nice stew beef. Among the secrets to preparing this quickly is using a store-bought, refrigerated pie crust. Pillsbury makes just such an item. You will need an aluminum foil pie pan for each serving—the size of the dish, of course, determines the size of the pie. For simplicity's sake, let's just go with a standard 8-inch pan.

> **2 cups cooked turkey, either white or dark meat, or chicken**
> **One 8-inch, store-bought refrigerated pie crust**
> **One 16-ounce package frozen green peas**
> **One 16-ounce package frozen carrots, either baby carrots or diced carrots**
> **One 16-ounce package cubed potatoes or even frozen steak fries, cut into cubes**

Quick Turkey Potpie

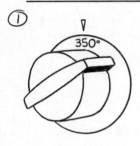

① 350°

②

③

④

⑤

⑥ 20:00

VARIATION:

**One 8-ounce can turkey gravy or the equivalent
from a larger package**

1. Preheat the oven or toaster oven to 350°F.
2. Spread the pie crust in and over the edges of an 8-inch pie pan.
3. In a large oven-proof bowl, and I stress "oven proof," combine the vegetables and gravy, and let defrost in your oven for 15 minutes. When defrosted and the gravy is hot, add the turkey or chicken and stir through until well blended.
4. Pour the mixture into the pie crust shell, fold the crust over the top, and bake for 30 minutes. Check the oven after 20 minutes to pierce the crust with a fork so the gravy can bubble over, and then make sure the top crust is browning. If too brown, cover the top of the pie loosely with aluminum foil and cook for another 10 minutes.
5. After 30 minutes, the pie should be ready. If it is still cool, return to the oven for another 10 minutes and keep checking for doneness.

Makes one 8-inch pie; serves 2 people, or 1 hungry person

VARIATIONS   Instead of using a store-bought pie crust, you can wrap individual serving pies in their dishes in a tortilla, corn or wheat, as if it's a crust, and prepare as above. For an enchilada pie, add hot pepper sauce to the turkey or chicken pie filling, spread shredded Mexican cheese over the pie before you cover with the tortilla, cover, and prepare as above.

If you like potpies, you can prepare mini potpies in small aluminum pie dishes in advance, or a larger pie in an 8-inch dish, keep covered or in the fridge until showtime, reheat, and serve in minutes.

Guacamole

For a fun variation on my turkey in pita, I sometimes like to add guacamole dip to the sandwich before I add the tomato and bean sprouts. Guacamole is also a great ingredient to add if you're building your turkey sandwich with bean sprouts on whole wheat or multigrain bread, either toasted or not.

Of course, you can buy premade guacamole in the supermarket. I do that all the time just to keep it in the refrigerator for whenever I want some nacho chips and guacamole dip. However, you can also make all kinds of tweaks to a basic guacamole recipe for your sandwich as well.

Accordingly, not to squeeze a dead avocado, here's my own tweak:

> 1 ripe avocado
> 1 teaspoon chili powder
> 1 teaspoon whole dried cumin seed, or 1 teaspoon
>   ground cumin
> Pinch of shredded cheddar and Monterey Jack
>   cheese (optional)
> Salt and freshly ground black pepper
> 3 to 5 drops Tabasco or your favorite hot sauce
>   (optional)
> Pinch of crushed red pepper flakes or cayenne
>   pepper (optional)

1. Split a ripe avocado in half, remove the pit, and reserve for replanting if you are in a climate that supports an avocado tree. Scoop out the fresh avocado pulp into a small mixing bowl. Press with a fork and turn until it is as smooth as you like. Lumps are OK if you like your guacamole chunky.

2. Add the chili powder and press into the mix with a fork, then stir through.

3. Place the whole cumin seed in the palm of your hand and, holding your hands over the avocado mixture, rub the cumin through your hand, grinding the seed over the mixture. This is the freshest form of cumin to use. If using ground cumin, then add the ground cumin to the avocado mixture.

4. Press the cumin into the mixture and stir with a fork. Add cheese, if using, and stir through. Season with salt and pepper to taste. Add hot sauce and crushed red pepper flakes to taste if you want to zap up the guacamole.

TO USE   When the guacamole is ready, simply eat it with a spoon or scoop a nacho chip through it. Or add it to your turkey in pita or spoon it onto a sandwich as a spread.

Makes 4 cups guacamole

English Toffee

Here's the secret of toffee: don't bite down hard, especially if you're over thirty-five and especially if you've had fillings or caps from root canal work. I once bit down into a piece of toffee while driving along Highland Boulevard in Hollywood and I really paid for it! If you're younger and have good strong teeth, you can bite, but you're still better off if you let the toffee melt in your mouth. You stuff it in the side of your mouth, like a baseball pitcher on the mound with chaw jammed into his cheek, and just let it melt right across your taste buds. The taste and warm afterglow of the sugar rush will last for hours. No wonder the British had an empire.

Melt your chocolate and chop your peanuts before you begin the recipe. Then you can assemble this layered toffee all at once, and enjoy.

> **1 cup chocolate chips, melted slightly, or 1 cup**
>   **Basic Chocolate Sauce (page 176)**
> **½ cup salted peanuts**
> **1 pound (4 sticks) butter**
> **2 cups sugar**

1. Melt the chocolate chips over very low heat or in a double boiler, or in a glass bowl set over a pot of simmering water. Finely chop the peanuts.

2. Cut the butter into small pieces and place in a heavy skillet with the sugar. Cook slowly over medium-high heat, stirring constantly, until the butter melts and is completely blended into the sugar.

3. Insert a candy thermometer into the mixture, reduce heat, and cook for 30 minutes, stirring constantly, until the mixture is a deep amber color and the thermometer registers 285°F. Pour the mixture into an ungreased baking sheet and allow to cool completely.

4. Spread the melted chocolate over the toffee and press the chopped peanuts on top. Place the entire dish in the refrigerator for at least 90 minutes, or longer if it is still warm to the touch, until the toffee sets and the chocolate hardens. When the chocolate has hardened, break the toffee into small pieces and store them in a tightly covered container.

Makes 18 ounces toffee

Tortoni

This may sound like a dessert in torts, but it's a classic Italian *dulce* that, in a traditional feast, is sometimes served to clear the palate for the next course. I like to make these tortoni well in advance, keep them on ice, and knock off one late at night. Sometimes I may even bring some to the studio for my crew. It's perfect for the long station breaks or during world news.

You will need fluted paper cups or small dessert cups for this traditional Italian delicacy.

> 1 large egg white
> 6 tablespoons Powdered Vanilla Sugar (page 180)
> 1 cup heavy cream
> ½ cup macaroon crumbs or Sweet Crumbs
> (page 47)
> 2 teaspoons rum
> ¼ cup chopped unsalted almonds

1. Using an electric mixer, beat the egg white until stiff peaks form and continue beating as you gradually fold in 3 tablespoons of the powdered vanilla sugar.
2. Using an electric mixer, beat the heavy cream with the rest of the powdered vanilla sugar until thick but not stiff. Mix the crumbs into the cream, add the rum, and beat until soft peaks form.
3. Fold the cream mixture into the egg whites, spoon into fluted paper cups or dessert cups, top with almonds, and freeze until firm.

Makes 2 cups or about 4 small tortoni

NOTE   I want to remind everyone about the inherent dangers of raw eggs. There was a time, back in the glorious 1950s when the Dodgers were still in Brooklyn, when you could find raw eggs in a lot of recipes. Even today you can use a raw egg as part of the preparation in a table-side Caesar salad. However, raw eggs, especially eggs that have not been refrigerated properly, do carry the danger of Salmonella, bacteria that cause food poisoning. The elderly, those with medical problems, people with allergies to eggs, and folks suffering from the flu should not consume raw eggs.

Honey Gelato

I've never considered myself a trendsetter or an especially cool guy. I like my Greek food, my Italian ices, and traditional home-made ice cream. But sometimes, especially in Los Angeles, someone will get you to try something new.

That's how I learned about this recipe. This is a trendy type of ice cream that is also good for you and, best of all, wonderfully low in calories. A ½-cup serving has 70 calories, so you can make up a batch and indulge without guilt.

> 1 envelope unflavored gelatin
> ½ cup instant nonfat dry milk
> 2 cups skim milk
> ½ cup honey
> 1 teaspoon fresh orange juice
> 1 teaspoon fresh lemon juice
> 2 large egg whites

1. Combine the gelatin and dry milk in a saucepan. Stir in the skim milk and cook over low heat, stirring constantly, until the gelatin dissolves. Remove from the heat.
2. Stir in the honey and juices. Pour the mixture into a freezer tray, a 9-inch cake pan, or ice cube tray and freeze for 1 hour.
3. Pour the mixture into a chilled bowl and add the egg whites. Beat at high speed with an electric mixer until the mixture is fluffy. Return to the freezer container, cover, and freeze until firm.

Makes 42 ounces gelato

NOTE Again, I want to remind everyone about the inherent dangers of raw eggs (see Note on page 94).

4

• CREATURES • MYTHS • LEGENDS •

Now's the time for some popcorn, some s'mores, and some campfire flashlights: It's story time! Let's listen to *Coast* favorite Lionel Fanthorpe weave a tale of undiscovered treasure.

We've had some fun with the recipes in this chapter. In honor of Linda Moulton Howe, the preeminent cattle mutilation expert, we present Alien Jerky, which is not as strange as it sounds.

Alien Jerky

Another school-yard favorite, especially when you want something quick to snack on without too much hassle, is beef jerky. I remember jerky from the 1950s, and trying to get the wrapper off so I could get a few chews in before getting off the school bus. I came up with my own recipe and still eat these in moderation.

This is also a great snack for hiking or for kids. Make up a batch of beef jerky if you want to keep your campers or hikers going for a long while. The concentrated flavor lasts and lasts as you chew, and since the cost of making this treat is so low, you can chew all day for pennies. Make up a batch in advance and savor it at your leisure.

1 pound very lean beef (chuck or round)
¼ cup Worcestershire sauce
¼ cup soy sauce
1 tablespoon tomato sauce
1 tablespoon vinegar
1 teaspoon sugar
¼ teaspoon dried onion (see page 54)
1 teaspoon salt
¼ teaspoon garlic powder

1. Trim all of the visible fat from the meat and freeze the meat until firm and solid enough to slice into thin strips. Cut across the grain, and make sure that the slices are as thin as you can make them, about ⅛ inch thick. Cut the slices into 1-inch-wide strips. Arrange the strips in a shallow baking pan.
2. Combine all of the remaining ingredients.

Alien Jerky

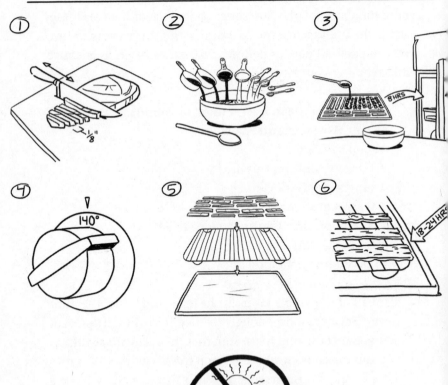

3. Pour the liquid over the strips. Refrigerate overnight or for at least 8 hours.

4. Preheat the oven to 140°F.

5. Remove the meat from the marinade and place the strips on a wire rack set over a baking sheet in the oven.

6. Dry until the strips will splinter on the edges, 18 to 24 hours. Cool completely before wrapping lightly with plastic wrap. The jerky will keep in a tightly covered container for 2 to 4 weeks.

Makes 32 ounces jerky

NOTE   Do not try to dry the meat in the sun, because you need a consistently higher temperature than the sun can provide. If you use a convection oven, you can reduce the drying time by 4 or 5 hours.

Boursin Party Spread

Everyone who tastes this cheese loves it. This version is easy to make, inexpensive, and even a little lower in calories than many of the popular, store-bought brands. Enjoy it with a dry white wine, crackers, slices of pepperoni, and white grapes. Serve as an appetizer or, again, just as an easy and relaxing snack late at night for radio listening.

½ cup cottage cheese
2 tablespoons butter, softened
2 tablespoons chopped fresh parsley
2 garlic cloves, pressed
1 teaspoon salt
1 teaspoon freshly ground black pepper

1. Drain the liquid from the cottage cheese in a cheesecloth-lined strainer suspended over a bowl for 1 to 2 hours. Discard the liquid.

2. In a food processor, blend the cheese and butter together until you have a smooth paste. Add the parsley, garlic, salt, and pepper, and blend well.

3. Shape the cheese into a ball and flatten the top. Chill for several hours, but remove from the refrigerator 1 hour before serving.

Makes 6 ounces spread

Open-Faced Turkey on Rye

You can use either rye or pumpernickel for this recipe, which is simply a variation of the leftover turkey sandwich, but this time open-faced, and something different. I like this because sometimes, if I am not in a rush and don't have to wrap up a sandwich to take to the studio, I indulge in a steamy open-faced sandwich that I can make in my own kitchen.

1 slice rye or pumpernickel bread
2 to 3 thick slices turkey, white or dark meat,
    your favorite portion
1 to 2 slices of Swiss or Muenster cheese
3 strips crisp, cooked bacon
2 to 3 tablespoons store-bought or leftover
    turkey gravy
2 slices tomato
Lettuce
Russian dressing, mustard, or mayonnaise, for
    serving

1. Place the slice of bread on a microwave-safe plate. Lay out the turkey meat, open-faced, over the slice of bread. Cover with the cheese. Lay the bacon strips over the cheese.
2. Spoon on the gravy and cover with tomato and lettuce. Top with your dressing or condiment of choice.
3. Microwave on high for 4 to 5 minutes, but not too long or the bread will harden.

Makes 1 sandwich

Open-Faced Quick Turkey and Mushroom Sandwich

By this time, you can figure out that not only do I like turkey (you can substitute sliced chicken for any of these sandwich recipes) but that I like turkey sandwiches. I actually like sandwiches of all kinds because, in my opinion, sandwiches are the perfect food.

Made right, a sandwich has everything you like. All you have to do is make sure that if you pick it up, stuff doesn't fall out and get all over you. Other than that, and especially if you don't care if the sandwich filling gets all over you, there's nothing to think about.

I also like open-faced sandwiches because you don't have to pick them up. Here's one of the easiest open-faced sandwiches you can make with store-bought ingredients right from the supermarket.

½ **can condensed mushroom soup, your favorite brand**
3 **to 4 turkey slices, your favorite portion**

1 slice pumpernickel or rye bread, or substitute
    a roll, whole wheat bread, or your favorite
    bread (I like the heft of pumpernickel myself)
Sliced tomato

1. Heat up the mushroom soup either in a saucepan on the stovetop or in the microwave for 3 to 5 minutes, just until it begins to bubble.
2. While the soup is heating, place your bread on a microwave-safe plate. Lay the turkey slices on the bread.
3. Spoon the heated mushroom soup onto your sandwich and place in the microwave for 90 seconds.
4. Remove from the microwave and let cool for 10 seconds, then cover with sliced tomato.

Makes 1 sandwich

Fast and easy, but it's a great late-night sandwich or a great lunch or quick dinner.

Gazpacho-Style Sauce

This is the Mexican-style version of Basic Tomato Sauce (page 27). Like its Italian and American counterparts, it can be frozen successfully and then slowly warmed or microwaved for use with tacos, enchiladas, Spanish-style rice, and various chicken and beef dishes.

2 medium onions, chopped
2 small green bell peppers, seeded and chopped
2 teaspoons corn oil

Two 20-ounce cans whole Italian plum tomatoes
   or 4 cups Basic Tomato Sauce (page 27) or
   4 pounds ripe plum or regular tomatoes
½ teaspoon salt
½ teaspoon freshly ground black pepper
½ teaspoon ground cumin
½ teaspoon chili powder
½ teaspoon dried oregano
¼ teaspoon cayenne pepper

1. In a pot over medium heat, brown the onion and bell pepper in the corn oil. Reduce the heat to low, and cook, stirring frequently, until the vegetables are soft and the onion is translucent.
2. If using canned tomatoes or Basic Sauce, stir into the oil mixture.
3. If using fresh tomatoes, blanch them in hot water. Transfer to cold water to cool down. When cool to the touch, peel them over the pot containing the oil mixture, discarding the skins, and drop in the whole tomatoes.
4. Season with salt and pepper and add the spices. Simmer, covered, for about 1 hour. Taste and adjust the seasonings, if needed.
5. The sauce can be stored, covered, in the refrigerator for about 1 week, or frozen for 3 to 9 months.

Makes 32 ounces sauce

George Noory's Special Caramel Ninja Turtles

You've all seen caramel turtles in the candy section of your supermarket. They taste great and you can savor them for a long time. When I was a kid, I would look forward to getting pecan- or walnut-covered caramel clusters from the real candy store down the street.

But late at night, when you have that need for a ninja turtle and everything is closed, where can you go? Answer: to your own kitchen. When I discovered the magic of this recipe, my baby boomer heart leapt for joy because it was like meeting up with an old friend once again.

Then, when I experimented and found the recipe to be so simple you could teach your kids to make it, I was even happier. My approach: they make it, I eat it. What could be simpler than that? These are my favorites. I unequivocally like these.

> 1 cup walnut or pecan pieces
> ½ cup caramel squares
> ½ cup shredded unsweetened coconut, but you
>   can add a pinch of sugar to taste
> ½ cup semisweet chocolate bits

1. Arrange the walnut or pecan pieces in clusters of four nut pieces each on a microwave-safe tray.
2. Cover each cluster with a single caramel square. Microwave the clusters you have just assembled for 1 minute on the medium setting, or until you see the caramel soften and spread over the nuts.

3. Remove from the microwave and sprinkle each cluster with shredded coconut. Return to the microwave and cook on medium for 30 seconds.

4. Remove from the microwave and, while still warm, place 2 chocolate bits on each cluster (representing the eyes), pressing them into the soft caramel.

5. Serve while still warm and chewy. You can also, which is what I do, eat one just to make sure you've done it right and set up your anticipation taste buds for when you eat these clusters as a late-night snack.

6. Refrigerate the clusters you have kept yourself from eating on the spot. You can eat them cold later on, or you can run to the kitchen, pull them out of the fridge, and microwave on low for 1 minute to make them soft and chewy again.

Again, call me on the air—not talking with your mouth full of caramel clusters—to tell me how much you enjoyed these.

Gimme Some More Stan's S'Mores

I know that you probably made these over an open fire at camp, listening to ghost stories, singing folk songs, slapping away mosquitoes that were eating you alive and getting all over your s'mores. I can smell the aroma of bug spray even now, mixed with the bouquet of chocolate and marshmallow. Now flash forward a couple of decades and here you are, listening to a great ghost story on *Coast*.

It's like the good old days all over again except that you're older, more settled, sitting on your couch, and with no bugs except in your computer. But you still have that old hankering for a s'more as you listen to my guest's description of a ghostly manifestation floating in the air or a strange voice from an abandoned old house. You really want a s'more. But where can you get one at one o'clock in the morning? In your kitchen, of course, by following this recipe.

> 10 graham crackers
> ½ cup crunchy peanut butter
> 5 chocolate squares or bars
> ½ cup Marshmallow Fluff

1. Lay out 5 single graham crackers on a microwave-safe tray. Spread each cracker with peanut butter and top with a chocolate square.
2. Top each chocolate-topped square with a spoonful of Marshmallow Fluff, then put another graham cracker on top.
3. Microwave all the graham crackers on low for 2 minutes, or until you can see the chocolate melting between the crackers.
4. Serve while still warm. You can save the rest, that is, if you can stay your hand from eating all of them, in the refrigerator and reheat in the microwave on low for 3 minutes.

Makes 5 s'mores

Frozen Banana Pops

These pops are a summertime favorite at our house. My grandkids like a mixture of vanilla and chocolate swirled together with lots of chocolate chips.

> ½ cup vanilla or chocolate Pudding Mix (page 182)

1 sliced banana
½ cup light cream
10 wooden sticks or Popsicle sticks

1. Prepare the pudding according to the directions and just before cooling, stir in the light cream and banana slices.
2. Pour the mixture into small cups or Popsicle molds and freeze until slushy, about 1 hour.
3. After 1 hour, insert the sticks and freeze until firm.

Makes 10 pops

VARIATION   To make a marbled pop, swirl ½ cup Basic Chocolate Sauce (page 176) into the vanilla pudding just before freezing. Don't mix the sauce in completely. Add chocolate chips, nuts, or butter-brickle chips, if desired.

5

• POP CULTURE • CURRENT EVENTS •
• ECONOMY •

Quick Coffee Cake

Soft Philly Pretzels

Orange-y Julius Drink

Homemade Cracker Jacks

Snackin' Jacks

The Classic Turkey Burger

Turkey Ball Hero or Hoagie

World's Best Turkey Club Sandwich

The Ultimate Thanksgiving Leftover Sandwich

Basic Turkey or Chicken Stew

Hot Ham and Cheese-its

Rainbow Drink Mix

Silly Saturday Cereal

We like to cover current events and breaking news on the show, but from a different perspective than you are likely to find on other radio shows. It's that difference that makes us unique, we think, and "unique" is the way I would describe many of the items in this chapter.

The bite of a big soft pretzel, which is unique to the East Coast, sends me right back to Philadelphia snackin' in my mind. All kinds of sweet popcorn remind me of my childhood and movie theaters, and when it's time for a more substantial meal, I like to turn to those foods unique to our culture here in the U.S.—club sandwiches, hoagies, and hot ham and cheese.

If news of the economy is getting you down, at least you can be sure that these recipes are thrifty. Leftovers are an American tradition in good times and bad, and there's no better leftover than stew, so as they say in England, keep calm and keep on.

Quick Coffee Cake

Sometimes the urge for something sweet comes over us as we're listening to our favorite guests on *Coast,* watching *UFO Hunters* or *Ancient Aliens* on television, or cruising the *UFO Magazine* blog online. A cup of coffee would be great. And a delicious coffee cake would be a great complement. But all the stores are closed.

What to do? Planning is the key. Make your coffee cake in advance, keep it in the fridge, and nuke it for a minute to heat it up while the coffee brews. But, if you want it fresher, this coffee cake takes no time to whip together. It can also be made even sweeter, depending on the amount of topping you crumble on.

CAKE
2 cups Biscuit Baking Mix (page 29)
½ cup sugar
1 large egg
1 cup whole milk
1 teaspoon Vanilla Bean Extract (page 205)

TOPPING
½ cup Biscuit Baking Mix (page 29)
½ cup lightly packed brown sugar
1 teaspoon ground cinnamon
2 tablespoons butter, softened

1. Preheat the oven to 350°F. Grease a 9-inch-square cake pan.
2. In a medium bowl, combine all of the ingredients for the coffee cake and beat well for 3 minutes with a wire whisk, an electric beater, or in a food processor. Pour into the prepared pan.

3. In a separate bowl, combine the ingredients for the topping and crumble them on top of the cake batter in the pan.

4. Bake for 20 to 25 minutes until a knife inserted in the center of the cake comes out clean.

Makes one 9-inch cake

Soft Philly Pretzels

These pretzels are one of the first things I remember about growing up—they were soft and chewy, and covered with salt—and some people liked them covered with mustard as well. Some Michiganers, of course, would never put mustard on them.

Mustard was only for the kids from Chicago, and cheese for the kids from Milwaukee, but everyone to his or her taste. You can reconstitute stale pretzels by sprinkling them with water, placing them in a paper bag, and heating in a 250-degree oven for 10 minutes or in a microwave for a minute or two.

> 1 envelope active dry yeast
> 1¼ cups warm water
> ¼ teaspoon sugar
> 2 teaspoons salt
> 4 to 5 cups all-purpose flour
> 4 teaspoons baking soda
> Coarse salt, for sprinkling

1. Dissolve the yeast in ¼ cup of the water and then stir in the remaining water and the sugar.

2. Pour the yeast mixture into a bowl, add the salt, and beat in enough flour to make a stiff dough. Knead by hand for 10 minutes, or until the dough is smooth and elastic. You can

Soft Philly Pretzels

perform this step using a food processor if you run the processor just until a ball of dough forms.

3. Add additional flour, a tablespoon at a time, to keep the dough from becoming too sticky. When the correct consistency is reached, continue to run the processor for another 60 seconds to knead the dough.

4. Place the dough in an oiled bowl, cover, and let rise for 45 minutes, or until doubled in bulk.

5. Turn the dough out onto a floured board and shape into pretzel shapes or fat sticks and twist a few times.

6. Preheat the oven to 475°F.

7. In a large pot, bring about 4 cups of water to a boil. Add 4 teaspoons of baking soda to the water. Drop in several pretzels at a time and boil for 1 minute, or until they float on the surface of the water. Using a skimmer, carefully remove the pretzels from the water and transfer to paper towels to drain.

8. Place the boiled pretzels on a greased baking sheet and sprinkle with coarse salt. Bake for 10 to 12 minutes until golden. Cool and store in a tightly closed container. The pretzels will keep for 2 to 4 weeks.

Makes 8 to 10 pretzels

Orange-y Julius Drink

There is a myth that the original Orange Julius contained ground eggshells because they can be whipped to a foamy mass. This version is tasty and light, sweet and foamy, but—no eggshells.

> 3 oranges, peeled and sliced
> 1 large egg

¼ cup sugar

1 teaspoon Vanilla Bean Extract (page 205)

6 ice cubes

Combine all of the ingredients in a blender and blend on high speed for a minute or two, or until frothy. Serve immediately.

Makes 24 ounces

VARIATION   Even though it doesn't have a famous name, a Lemon Julius, made with 3 lemons, is delicious, too.

NOTE   Remember that raw eggs, especially eggs that have not been refrigerated properly, do carry the danger of Salmonella, a food poisoning. The elderly, those with medical problems, people with allergies to eggs, and folks suffering from the flu should not consume raw eggs.

Homemade Cracker Jacks

Following along the same logic that we sometimes need some guilty pleasure munchies to get the conversation going about a controversial guest and the guest's opinions—such as a Richard Hoagland suggestion that he be made the DiMrector of NASA—a sweet treat to mellow out the mood is in order.

Here's a recipe for the snack we all grew up on, but are probably too old to indulge in now. Once in a while, though, it doesn't hurt.

A candy thermometer is handy to have for this recipe to test the temperature of the syrup that binds the popcorn and nuts together.

4 cups popped corn
1 cup shelled peanuts
½ cup molasses
¼ cup sugar

1. Mix the popcorn and peanuts together in a large bowl or pan.
2. Cook the molasses and sugar together until the mixture reaches a temperature of 235°F on a candy thermometer. If you don't have a thermometer, test the syrup by dropping some from a spoon into a cup of cold water; the syrup is done when it forms a thread as it drops into the water.
3. Pour the hot syrup mixture over the popcorn-nut mixture and stir to coat evenly. Cool and break into chunks with a wooden spoon. Stored in an airtight container, the mixture will keep well for 4 to 6 weeks.

Makes 6 cups Homemade cracker jacks

Snackin' Jacks

Now we're getting serious. When the late-night doldrums strike and you feel as if you need something, anything, to pull you through or send you off to sleep with that feeling of intense guilty pleasure at having consumed a sinfully delicious treat, this is the recipe for you.

As its name so artfully implies, there is a candy-store vending machine brand you can buy. But if you make it yourself, it's fresher, cheaper, and, because you don't have all that wrapping to dispose of, eco-friendly.

You will probably want to make this in advance of your late-night hunger pangs. And because this is a microwave specialty, I recommend that you use microwave popcorn, which you can get in any supermarket. You can certainly use popcorn that you buy in large bags, but it will lack some of the freshness that you might want for your Snackin' Jacks.

Even better, and what I use because I like popcorn, especially caramel-coated popcorn, so much, get yourself a microwave popcorn popper. They're easy to use and will do the job just as well as one of those electric old-time movie theater poppers. A microwave popcorn popper also will save you money on your not having to buy popcorn in bags, which you can easily overpop and might even set on fire if you let it go for too long.

> 1 cup tightly packed brown sugar
> ¼ cup (½ stick) butter or margarine
> ¼ cup light corn syrup
> ½ teaspoon salt
> ½ teaspoon baking soda
> 15 cups popped popcorn

1. Mix the sugar, butter, syrup, and salt in a microwave-safe bowl and cook on high until the butter is completely melted and bubbly and you can see that the ingredients are thoroughly blended.
2. Remove the bowl from the microwave and stir in the baking soda. Divide the popped corn between two microwave-safe sheets, and pour half the sugar mixture over each, stirring the popcorn as you pour.
3. Microwave the sheets on high for 5 minutes, rotate, and microwave for another 5 minutes. Let cool before you dive in.
4. You can store your Snackin' Jacks in an airtight container, or separate into individual servings and either store or eat them right up. This treat will keep for at least 2 weeks.

◆ **Snackin' Jacks with Peanuts:** You can also add a cup or two of dry-roasted, shelled peanuts to your popcorn mixture before you coat it with the sweet stuff. And if you really want to send yourself to the ceiling with the joy of taste, try mixing up one of the batches with melted American or cheddar cheese in addition to the butter when you're mixing up the sweet coating. You will then have your own version of a cheesie snackin'. Eat it up late at night and make sure you hit the gym the next day.

Here's an idea that your neighbors will probably get nervous about unless you let them know about it first. Tell your neighbors about this recipe. Spread the word and tell them that you'll be making up little Halloween treat bags with Snackin' Jacks. That way, you get to hand out individualized bags of goodies to the trick-or-treaters without incurring the frothing wrath of their overzealously ego-challenged parents. Just sayin'.

The Classic Turkey Burger

Turkey burgers are a great alternative to all-beef hamburgers, just like lamb burgers are a great alternative. You can buy frozen ground turkey patties in the store, of course, throw them on the grill, and put them on a bun.

But, if you have the time, or, as I do, make them up in advance for a late-night dinner, you can always have them on hand, made to order. Here's one of my favorite recipes that you can vary depending on the different kind of soup mixes you want to add for flavor.

1 pound fresh ground turkey

¼ cup tomato or vegetable juice or, for an extra
   kick, Bloody Mary mix

½ cup bread crumbs or stuffing mix, ground
   fine (optional if you want to stretch the
   amount of turkey meat)

½ packet flavored dried onion or mushroom
   soup mix (your favorite brand)

2 to 3 drops Tabasco or your favorite hot sauce

Salt and freshly ground black pepper

1 teaspoon olive or vegetable oil

1 small garlic clove, thinly sliced

½ small onion, sliced

1 package favorite buns or potato rolls

1 small to medium ripe tomato, sliced

1. In a medium bowl, knead the ground turkey to soften it. Add half of the tomato or vegetable juice, then gradually add the bread crumbs or stuffing mix, kneading all the time to blend the ingredients. As you knead, add the remaining juice, or more, as needed. You are blending as well as softening the turkey meat.

2. When all of the bread crumbs and juice have been blended with the turkey meat, slowly add the dried soup mix, again, kneading it through to blend in the dried soup thoroughly.

3. Add the Tabasco or your favorite hot sauce. Season lightly with salt and pepper.

4. Heat the oil in a large skillet over high heat, add the garlic, and cook until it begins to brown. Add the onion and cook until translucent.

5. Form the turkey mixture into bun-size patties, large or small depending on your proclivity, on a large plate.

6. Immediately place the patties in the skillet, pressing down

gently with a spatula to flatten them, while turning over the onions and garlic. Turkey patties, being poultry meat, should be cooked medium to medium well, not rare.

7. Transfer them to a separate plate to drain. Split the rolls and briefly press them into the oil, garlic, and onion mix to grill them very quickly.

8. Transfer the rolls to serving plates, fill each with a patty, top with sliced tomato, and serve.

Makes 4 to 6 burgers depending on the size of the patties

VARIATIONS

✦ **Bacon-Turkey Burgers:** Here are some easy toppings. You can make bacon-turkey burgers by frying the bacon first in the skillet before you add the oil, garlic, and onions. Transfer the cooked bacon to paper towels to drain. Drain off most of the bacon fat from the skillet, then add the oil, garlic, and onions and continue to prepare as above. Top each patty with one or two slices of bacon.

✦ **Turkey Cheeseburgers:** You can also have turkey cheeseburgers, using your favorite sliced cheese, with or without bacon. Just add the cheese slices while the turkey patties are still cooking, but almost done.

✦ **Avocado or Guacamole Burgers:** Another serving variation that I like is avocado or guacamole. You can either prepare the guacamole mix, as on page 90, or you can split a ripe avocado and spoon the meat onto your patty as a topping either with the cheese and bacon or without.

✦ **Other toppings for burgers:** Try ketchup, salad dressing, olive oil and vinegar, or even blue cheese dressing, they are all up to your own taste.

Turkey Ball Hero or Hoagie

For this recipe you will need soft torpedo rolls for the sandwiches; I prefer those imported from Philly. You will also need a sauce. I like a spicy tomato sauce the best, especially a tomato sauce made from New Jersey tomatoes, but any basic tomato sauce is easily spiced up with crushed red pepper flakes.

Make the meatballs according to the recipe for Turkey Meatballs (page 253). Or, if you have made them in advance, use your refrigerated or frozen Turkey Meatballs.

In the hoagie shops in Trenton and South Philly, including Chester, the sandwich-makers like to split the meatballs so they can wrap the sandwiches more easily. But follow your own taste.

> 16 ounces tomato sauce, spiced with a pinch of
>   crushed red pepper flakes (optional)
> 12 Turkey Meatballs (page 253)
> Four 6-inch soft torpedo rolls
> 1 teaspoon olive oil (optional)
> Pinches of dried oregano
> Pinches of dried parsley
> Pinches of dried basil (optional)
> 1 to 2 slices provolone or mozzarella cheese per
>   serving or ⅓ cup shredded provolone or
>   mozzarella cheese per serving

1. In a small saucepan on the stovetop or in a microwave, heat the tomato sauce. If using cooked refrigerated or frozen meatballs, warm them in the tomato sauce until heated through.
2. Split the rolls, sprinkle with olive oil, if that's your pleasure, and spoon on some of the tomato sauce. After the

sauce has soaked into the bread, lay on the meatballs, as many as you think you can fit.

3. Spoon on more sauce, a little oregano, parsley, and maybe some basil. Top with your slices of cheese or shredded cheese, and put the sandwich back in the oven, or in the microwave, just until the cheese melts.

Makes four medium, 6-inch hero sandwiches

VARIATIONS

◆ **Open-Faced Meatball Sandwiches:** How about this variation, open-faced meatball sandwiches on torpedo rolls or soft kaiser rolls, seeded or unseeded? Use the same method of preparation as above, but this time, don't fold over the roll or cover the sandwich with the top portion of bread. Sprinkle with olive oil, spoon on the heated tomato sauce, cover each of the two sides of the roll with the meatballs, either whole, split, or flattened, spoon on more sauce, add the spices, top with the cheese slices, and heat until the cheese melts. Remove from the oven and serve.

Whether you're enjoying these freshly made or whether you've made them in advance and refrigerated or frozen them, these sandwiches hit the spot, especially at late-night listening sessions. Your friends, if you have them over for a *Coast* party, will certainly appreciate the care you've taken to prepare this dish.

◆ **Turkey Meatballs Cocktail Style:** One of the things my friends told me they used to enjoy were the happy hours at the Ivy League clubs in New York. You could relax there at Harvard, Yale, Columbia, or Princeton clubs, sit back, and enjoy plates of cocktail meatballs in a delightful gravy sauce.

You don't need an Ivy League degree to pop these little turkey ball beauties into your mouth after a hard day's work or during a relaxing, spiritual conversation on *Coast*. Simply roll your ground turkey meat (see Turkey Meatballs, page 253) into tiny meatballs and cook them in whatever sauce you choose, turkey gravy or tomato sauce.

Heat up a second plate or bowl of sauce in a saucepan or in your microwave. Season the turkey balls with salt and pepper to taste. Serve the turkey balls in the heated sauce to your friends, and let them savor the flavor.

◆ **Turkey Meatball Pizza:** We have basic pizza recipes, but I wanted to add one variation here. Follow the recipe above, using either an English muffin or a kaiser roll and soak it with olive oil, spread with tomato sauce, season with some dried oregano, garlic, and basil, and heat in a microwave for 2 minutes on high, or in your toaster oven at 400°F for 5 minutes. Using some of those nice and spicy turkey meatballs you've made, top off your homemade pizza, sprinkle with a little Parmesan cheese, reheat, and you have a fresh, homemade turkey ball pizza.

World's Best Turkey Club Sandwich

The original Sunday brunch at the golf or yacht club, this sandwich, usually made with three slices of toasted bread—whole wheat or white—so as to make it a double-decker, which is then quartered, is a staple. It's a basic combination of turkey, bacon, Swiss cheese, if you like, lettuce, tomato, and a variety of salad dressings ranging from straight mayonnaise to a combination of mustard and mayo or a variety of spices. I'm always partial to cilantro myself. You might ask, though, what makes this a club sandwich? Good question.

The history of this dish is not a mysterious conspiracy, but different food historians have different opinions. One story says that the club sandwich was invented by a chef in the 1890s working up in the Adirondacks in New York. The sandwich became so popular that it began turning up in restaurants in New York City at the turn of the century and from there spread across the country. Today, you can find hoagie, grinder, submarine, hero, or torpedo roll versions of the turkey club at sandwich and fast-food shops across the country. You can even find a turkey club bagel.

I am a late-night talk-show host working in the tradition of Long John Nebel and Art Bell. As such, I can't let something like the word "hoagie" or "hero" sandwich go by without just a word or two of explanation. Read to eat. Read to learn.

Most food historians agree that the term "hoagie," an Italian sandwich filled with sliced meat such as capicola, prosciutto, or other spiced ham, provolone, hot or sweet peppers, tomato, olive oil, and vinegar, was first used during World War I in a place called Hog Island in south Philadelphia, the home of a shipyard. The yard workers and dockworkers, most of whom were Italian immigrants, created the lunch box sandwich, which became known as the "hoagie" after Hog Island.

In other versions of the story, the people who ate these humongous stuffed sandwiches on long rolls were supposedly the workers on Hog Island and were referred to as "Hoggies." The name became applied to the sandwich itself, which was renamed the "hoagie." And in still another version of the story, the sandwich was made in a luncheonette in good old Chester, Pennsylvania, that served the workers of Hog Island and became known as "the hoagie." But no matter what version of the story you like, the real secret of the hoagie is the long roll, the hoagie version of which was baked in Chester or South Philly and is unmatched for its softness and flavor. Must be the water.

The term "grinder" has a similar history, although not from Philadelphia, but from Boston. According to history, when the first Italian workers came to the United States, settling in northeastern cities, many of them were quickly hired as stone-cutters and tile cutters. If you ever have the chance to travel to Princeton, New Jersey, especially the Princeton University campus, you will see some of the most artistic stonework on the East Coast. This was the work of the Italian stonemasons and slate workers who came here during the nineteenth century. In Boston, the workers who built their huge Italian meat and cheese and pepper sandwiches on long rolls also used grinding machines to join pieces of stone and slate. Hence, they were referred to as "grinders," and that became the name of their sandwich rolls and sandwiches.

The names for "torpedo roll" and "submarine sandwich" are almost obvious because of the long shape of the roll, but the name "hero," commonly associated with the long roll sandwich in New York City and its suburbs, is another matter.

A common misconception of the hero sandwich is that it took a hero to eat the whole thing. But that's probably not true. My explanation, probably because I am an avid devotee of Greek food, is that the sandwich, although popular in New York in the 1950s, got the name "hero" attached to it from the Greek, *gyro,* a shaved meat sandwich on a pita-type roll.

You can see gyro stands all over New York City. The word *gyro* in Greek is pronounced not with the same initial sound as the name John, but with a consonant similar to the sound of an *h* but articulated all the way in the front of the mouth almost directly behind the hard palate. Greek *y* sounds just like the vowel in the word "we." Hence, the name of the modern English "hero" sandwich, according to the George Noory unofficial history of fast foods.

> 2 slices of your favorite bread, usually lightly toasted
> Extra-virgin olive oil
> 3 to 4 thin slices turkey, either homemade or store-bought

2 to 3 strips cooked, crisp bacon

2 leaves lettuce

2 slices fresh tomato

Pinch of salt, cayenne or paprika, dried oregano,
    and garlic powder

Mayonnaise, Cilantro Mayonnaise (page 153), or
    Mustard Mayonnaise (page 284)

1. Toast the bread, or not, spread the slices very lightly with extra-virgin olive oil, and build your sandwich with all the above ingredients. Place the sandwich on a microwave-safe plate.
2. Microwave for 30 seconds, remove, and cut the sandwich into quarters, cutting off the crust, if that's your pleasure, and serve.

Makes 1 sandwich

The Ultimate Thanksgiving Leftover Sandwich

It's the night after Thanksgiving when all are asleep and you are all alone by the radio listening to *Coast*. Suddenly, even after all that turkey the night before, you have a craving—a craving for something ultimate, something to bring back the excitement of the night before when the turkey sat happily on the dinner table oohed and aahed by hungry, wide-eyed family and friends. Here's my dish, the Thanksgiving leftover sandwich. It is a five-minute meal sure to satisfy not only your late-night hunger but your remembrance of Thanksgivings past, especially the one the night before.

Thickly sliced leftover cooked turkey, your
favorite portions
Hoagie or grinder roll
Heaping scoop of leftover stuffing
2 tablespoons cranberry sauce
1 or more slices Swiss or American cheese
2 to 3 teaspoons leftover turkey gravy or
substitute canned gravy

1. Lay out the turkey slices on your roll. You can substitute a kaiser or another soft roll if hoagie or grinder rolls aren't available. You can also use a soft onion roll or a kaiser with poppy seeds.
2. Heat the stuffing in the microwave for 15 seconds to soften. Spread the stuffing onto the sandwich.
3. Add cranberry sauce to taste and then one or more slices of cheese to taste.
4. Place the sandwich on a microwave-safe plate. Spoon over the gravy and heat in the microwave for 90 to 120 seconds.

Makes 1 sandwich

Basic Turkey or Chicken Stew

Just like many of the other turkey recipes, a basic stew has scores of variations. This is a recipe you will make in advance, just like the turkey chili, refrigerate or freeze, and keep on hand for either a sumptuous dinner with lots of soft biscuits, a late brunch with stew over toast points, or that late-night snack with a nice soft roll you can dunk into the stew or use to sop up the stew gravy.

1 teaspoon olive or vegetable oil

2 to 3 cups cooked, cubed turkey or chicken

1 medium sliced onion

One 16-ounce package frozen peas

One 16-ounce package frozen sliced green beans
(optional)

6 baby carrots, washed and diced, or one
16-ounce package frozen diced carrots

1 cup all-purpose flour

3 cups store-bought chicken broth or bouillon

2 cups store-bought turkey or chicken gravy

1 cup water

6 small red potatoes, peeled and cubed

2 teaspoon dried parsley

1 teaspoon dried rosemary

1 teaspoon dried thyme

1 tablespoon dried sage, if you have it, or you
can use poultry seasoning

1 bay leaf

1. In a large saucepan, heat the olive oil and add the turkey or chicken to brown, stirring constantly. Add the onion. Cook until translucent.

2. Stir the flour into the meat and onion mixture. Let cook for 1 to 2 minutes.

3. Add the bouillon, gravy, and 1 cup water, and stir until the mixture thickens. Add the potatoes.

4. Add the frozen vegetables and fresh carrots, if using, and stir. Cover and let cook on the stovetop over very low heat for 1 hour.

5. Add the parsley, rosemary, thyme, sage or poultry seasoning, and bay leaf and cook for 15 to 30 minutes over low heat to allow the herbs to flavor the stew. Remove and discard the bay leaf before serving.

Makes 6 to 8 servings

VARIATIONS   You can pour the stew into small aluminum pie pans or inside tortilla shells, and bake at 350°F for 30 minutes.

You can serve the stew over toast or over biscuits or hot rolls.

You can save leftovers or add half-and-half or light cream to make cream of turkey or chicken soup.

Hot Ham and Cheese-its

OK, who likes Cheese-its? I see lots of hands out there in *Coast to Coast* land. Now, if I told you that in the space of five minutes you can make even better Cheese-its, Cheese-its piping hot with ham, who would like that? Me, too. I like that. In fact, it's something I make for myself no matter where I'm broadcasting from.

I have to tell you, this recipe is so deceptively simple that I don't know why you can't find it in fast-food restaurants across the country. Their loss is our gain, especially when you can make this recipe for pennies per Cheese-it.

> 8 slices ham, either store-bought or home
>   cooked, thinly sliced
> 4 slices white bread
> 2 teaspoons mayonnaise
> ½ teaspoon mustard, hot or plain (optional)
> 4 slices American cheese
> 1 small tomato, thinly sliced

1. Arrange individual slices of ham on a microwave-safe tray and microwave for 1 minute. Transfer the ham slices to a plate and set aside.

2. Microwave the slices of bread for 30 seconds. Top each slice of bread with 2 slices of ham, and spread with mayonnaise. You can mix the mustard with the mayonnaise for a sharper taste. Top with a slice of cheese.

3. Microwave for 1 minute, or until the cheese melts. Top each slice with a slice of tomato and microwave again for 45 seconds.

4. You can either cut the bread slices into small squares, roll them up, and pop 'em in like Cheese-it snacks, or eat the entire slice, sandwich style. You should eat them while still hot, but you can also store them in your fridge and wrap them in aluminum foil for your own or your kids' lunch boxes and eat them cold. These are versatile and friendly treats that satisfy any late-night munchy desires.

Makes 4 sandwiches or 16 Cheese-its

Rainbow Drink Mix

Drop a tablespoon or two of this mix into your milk and watch the milk turn a pretty shade of pink, yellow, blue, or green.

You may think the drink is fun, but you will have added a nice nutritional boost as well. You can also use this mix to make Silly Saturday Cereal (page 133) as an alternative to the coated cereals that you grew up with, or in spite of them.

2 cups instant nonfat dry milk
¼ cup Silly Sparkles (page 276)
2 tablespoons protein powder
1 teaspoon Powdered Vanilla Sugar (page 180)

Combine all of the ingredients and store in an airtight canister or a tightly covered jar for up to 4 months. Stir well before using.

TO USE   For fortified milk, add 1 to 2 tablespoons of the mix to a glass of cold milk, place in a jar, cover, and shake vigorously. Or place the milk and mix in a blender and whirl on high speed for 1 minute.

Add a teaspoon or two to hot cereal, add a splash of cold milk, and swirl to make a marble pattern with a spoon.

Makes 19 ounces mix

VARIATIONS   For yellow or orange milk, add 1 tablespoon grated orange zest or 1 teaspoon grated lemon zest to the mix.

For green milk, add 1 teaspoon dried mint leaves, ground fine between two spoons, to the mix.

For pink milk and sophisticated children, add 1 teaspoon dried rose petals, ground fine, to the mix.

Silly Saturday Cereal

Make up a batch of this cereal for one of the shows for the weekend. The cereal is best eaten right away—serve with cold milk and sliced fresh fruit. Extra cereal can be stored in an airtight container for another time or eaten as a snack.

½ cup Rainbow Drink Mix (page 132)
2 tablespoons honey, warmed
2 cups plain wheat, corn, or rice cereal
½ cup chopped dried fruit
½ cup miniature marshmallow bits

1. Combine the Rainbow Drink Mix with the warmed honey. Pour over the cereal and toss until the cereal is completely covered.
2. Stir in the fruit and marshmallows and serve.

Makes 16 ounces mix

6

• MYSTERIES • ANOMALIES •

Crepes Diem

Blintzes

Chewie Cheesies

Your Favorite Croutons

Cheesy Soup Croutons

Croutons Calabrese

Quick Chicken Liver Pâté

Turkey Pesto

Curried Turkey or Chicken Sloppy Joes

Gingerbread Puzzles

Cilantro Mayonnaise

Schmageggies

What greater mystery can there be than the alchemy that takes place between expectation and fork? Part of the fun of our show is never knowing where we might go with a conversation or an idea.

Mystery is the spice of life, after all. Most of the recipes in this chapter are a little out there, a little bit mysterious, and all of them are taste surprises—croutons that come alive and invigorate soup, pesto and curry and cilantro, and what in the heck? Schmageggies?

Crepes Diem

Let's say there are no aliens on the horizon, at least for tonight, so you want to make something other than pancakes. (See Quick Mabel, the Pancakes! on page 252.) Now you can relax and make some thin, sophisticated all-American crepes.

Making crepes can be easy if you already have a batch of Biscuit Baking Mix (page 29) in the pantry. You may have to practice a bit to get the hang of flipping and filling the crepes, but after a little experimentation, you should be able to make crepes very quickly. Make sure the pan you use is hot enough to make a drop of water bounce merrily on the surface, and make sure the pan is smooth, with no rough spots.

Crepes can be filled with various meat stuffings for a quick dinner or brunch, and they are fantastic with sliced fruits for dessert. Top a sweetened crepe with a tablespoon of liqueur for a fancy, grown-up taste, and check the variations here for additional ways to fill and serve your crepes.

You can make a big batch of crepes at one time, cool them, and then freeze with a sheet of wax paper or plastic wrap between each one for even quicker suppers and desserts.

> 2 cups Biscuit Baking Mix (page 29)
> 1½ cups whole milk
> 4 large eggs

1. Combine all of the ingredients in a blender, food processor, bowl, or shaker container and mix until smooth. The batter will be thin.
2. In a crepe pan or an 8-inch sloped-sided pan, preferably nonstick, heat the butter.

3. For each crepe, pour about ¼ cup of the batter into the hot pan. Turn the pan until the batter coats the bottom in a thin sheet. Cook over medium heat until golden brown. Loosen the edge of the crepe with a spatula, turn over, and cook the other side until golden brown. Repeat with the remaining batter.

4. To reheat frozen crepes, either thaw them, still wrapped, at room temperature for 1 hour before warming in an oven set to 350°F, or unwrap and place in a microwave oven on medium for 1 or 2 minutes.

Makes 12 crepes

VARIATIONS

◆ **Savory Dinner or Brunch Crepes:** Try filling crepes with a spoonful of finely ground tuna, chicken, or turkey salad and top with white sauce.

◆ **Dessert Crepes:** Fill crepes with spiced apples, sweetened cherries, or berries, top with sweetened whipped cream, and dust with ground cinnamon.

Blintzes

Remember the scene in *The Godfather: Part II* (1974) when Frankie "Five Fingers" complains that the chopped liver crackers he's eating are called canapés? Think of blintzes as crepes in reverse, only with sour cream instead of powdered sugar.

BATTER
2 cups Biscuit Baking Mix (page 29)
1½ cups whole milk
2 tablespoons sugar

1 teaspoon Vanilla Bean Extract (page 205)
4 large eggs

FILLING
1 cup Homemade Cream Cheese (page 44) or
  store-bought cream cheese
2 tablespoons Powdered Vanilla Sugar (page
  180), plus more for dusting
¼ cup sour cream

1. Mix the batter and cook the blintzes, as instructed for the crepes (see previous recipe).
2. Mix the cream cheese with the sugar. Fill each crepe, while still warm, with the sweetened cream cheese, top with sour cream, and dust with more sugar.

Makes 12 blintzes

Chewie Cheesies

Remember the good old days before you had to think about cholesterol, weight gain, trans fats, chemical additives and preservatives, and shopping in the supermarket with a magnifying glass at the ready so you can see what's in the stuff you buy? The good old days, when nobody scolded you for eating too much sugar, too much starch, too much salt, and too much sodium benzoate, may be gone but are not forgotten.

The good old days when a glowing green flying saucer was just landing over the hill and Stanton Friedman had not yet encountered retired major Jesse Marcel in Louisiana and Frankie Rowe was still wrestling with her knowledge that we had been visited by beings from another world who left debris on a rancher's field outside of Roswell—material that she, herself, handled.

Those good old days in Detroit when Chryslers had tail fins bigger than a 747, the world was aghast when the new Chevies came out with dual headlights, and a Ford Fairlane 500 had an engine so big it would drain your gas tank when you stepped on the accelerator. Gas, by the way, was 23 cents a gallon right off the exit for the Throgs Neck Bridge in Queens. Those were the days when the music sound coming out of Detroit was so new, so different, you knew that a happier world had arrived. Those were the days.

In those days you could eat chewie or crunchy cheese sticks with abandon, anytime you wanted, and even have them in your school lunch box. Guess what? Those days are back with my healthy, microwave-prepared chewie cheese sticks created just for you. Make them up in advance, vary the recipe with different types of cheddar cheese from store-bought to that wonderful hunk of cheddar you get at the whole earth farmers' market. Think beautiful downtown Venice, California, on a Friday morning or sunny Santa Monica or even Manhattan's Union Square or the Old Country: Brooklyn. Here's how to make them:

> 1 cup all-purpose flour
> 1 teaspoon salt (or kosher salt if you want to
>   blow off your tongue)
> 1 teaspoon paprika
> 2 cups grated cheddar cheese
> ¼ cup (½ stick) butter (salted or unsalted, your
>   choice)

1. Sift the flour, salt, and paprika together into a medium bowl. Stir in the grated cheddar cheese.

2. In a food processor, or using a handheld electric mixer, cream the butter until light and fluffy.

3. Slowly add the flour-and-cheese mixture to the creamed butter and continue mixing until the ingredients are thoroughly blended.

4. Remove the mixture from the bowl and shape into a long roll, about 2 inches in diameter. Twist the ends to seal. Wrap the roll in wax paper, and store in the refrigerator overnight.

5. The next day, remove the roll from the refrigerator and cut the chilled dough into very thin slices. Place the slices on a microwave-safe sheet or paper plate.

6. Roll and twist the individual slices into crescents and place in the microwave.

7. Microwave the slices for 3 minutes on high, rotate the dish, and microwave again for 2 minutes on medium.

8. Remove the crescents from the microwave and allow to cool on your countertop until they are set. Chill them in the refrigerator for 1 to 2 days. When set and cooled, these snacks can be stored anywhere, though refrigerating is best because there are no preservatives.

Makes 24 servings

Your Favorite Croutons

Remember when we used croutons in our earlier recipes with turkey or chicken? You can always buy croutons at the store. However, if you really—and I mean really—like croutons just as snacks as well as in soups and salads and can never have enough in the house? Why worry and run to the market every five minutes, burning gas and getting strange looks from the checkout people? Make them yourself by the bagful by reusing old bread and doing a basic recycle.

The great part about making your own croutons, and keeping them on hand for any recipes calling for croutons, is that you can make them in different flavors for your different dishes. Croutons all by themselves are delightful snacks, a great substitute for bagel chips, and go with you anywhere. Whenever I make up a batch, I like to bring a bag of them to the studio to nibble on the way.

If you store these croutons in a tightly sealed container in your refrigerator, they keep for a very long time. Also, whenever you want to refresh your crouton stash, just make more and add them to the storage container—the new croutons will enhance the flavor of the ones you've kept in storage.

Croutons, besides being the great additions to salads and soups, also serve as a snappy topping to any of your potato dishes, including scalloped potatoes, twice-baked potatoes, and even mashed potatoes. These croutons can also become the basis of your Thanksgiving turkey stuffing, stuffing for roasted chicken or duck, and stuffed pork chops.

By varying the type of cheese or spices, you can add crunch and more taste to any meal calling for stuffing. In fact, if you like stuffed cod or any other type of fish fillet that can stand up to being rolled and stuffed, you will be especially happy about this recipe. It's a late-night snack that is a meal in itself, made in a jiffy.

> 1 cup day-old rolls, cubed
> 2 tablespoons butter, salted
> 1 teaspoon seasoned salt: garlic, onion, and/or
>   celery salt
> 1 teaspoon dried herbs: your choice of thyme,
>   tarragon, or poultry seasoning

½ teaspoon paprika
¾ cup grated cheddar cheese

1. In a microwave-safe dish, melt the butter for 2 minutes on high.
2. Stir the seasoned salt, grated cheese, dried herbs of your choice, and paprika into the dish of melted butter. Spread out the bread cubes in another dish, pour the butter mixture over the cubes, and toss thoroughly to make sure that each cube is coated with the butter mixture.
3. Microwave the croutons on high for 5 minutes, remove from the microwave, shake the croutons, and rotate the tray. Microwave for 2 minutes more. Repeat the rotating and shaking and microwave for one more 2-minute cycle.
4. When the final cycle is complete, remove the croutons from the microwave and set aside to cool.
5. Once cool, you can eat them right up, use them in recipes calling for stuffing or breaded topping, or store them in the fridge for snacking. The croutons will keep for at least 2 months in the refrigerator. If you want to replenish your supply, just add new croutons to the container and make sure you shake the container vigorously to distribute the spices and seasonings evenly.

Makes 2 cups croutons

VARIATIONS
◆ **Bacon Croutons:** Cook up 3 or more slices of bacon by placing them on a microwave-safe plate between sheets of paper towels. Microwave on high until the bacon browns and crisps. Remove from the microwave and transfer to fresh paper towels to drain and cool. Crumble the bacon strips into your crouton container and shake vigorously. Let sit for 1 hour, and you have

bacon-flavored croutons for your salads and potato toppings.

◆ **Bacon and Onion Croutons:** Want even more flavor? In a small skillet, brown up a small onion in butter or olive oil. When brown, microwave it for 2 minutes on paper towels, drain, crumble, and add it to the bacon crumbles before mixing it with the croutons. Wow! Who needs to put this on anything? Just eat it.

◆ **Italian Croutons:** Use aged, imported provolone in place of the cheddar, but make sure it's on the sharp side.

Cheesy Soup Croutons

These little beauties will turn any regular mug of soup into something special. For something very light late at night, I heat up some water, mix it with bouillon cubes, drop in a few croutons, and I have a real treat that holds me over until breakfast.

> 1 cup cubed day-old bread
> 1 tablespoon melted butter
> Pinch of oregano
> Pinch of dried crushed hot red pepper
> Pinch of salt
> ½ cup grated or shredded Parmesan cheese

1. Pour the melted butter over the bread cubes in a large bowl.
2. Add the spices and toss thoroughly.
3. Add the cheese and toss.
4. Spread out the bread-cube mixture on a shallow microwave-safe sheet or baking dish and microwave, as in previous recipe, for 5 minutes. Shake the pan and rotate and microwave for another 2 minutes. Let cool before eating, and refrigerate to store.

Makes 6 1-cup servings

South o' the Border Croutons

½ cup cubed day-old bread
½ cup nacho chips, flavored or unflavored, your
    choice, crumbled
½ teaspoon each chili powder, ground cumin,
    and dried oregano
½ cup shredded cheddar and Jack cheese mixture
1 tablespoon corn oil

Follow the basic steps of mixing, seasoning, and microwaving croutons as in the main recipe. Enjoy as a very zesty crouton snack, a topping for tortilla soup, or a topping for a great avocado salad.

Makes 6 servings

Croutons Calabrese

These are great for turning regular leaves of lettuce and a few onion slices into pseudo Caesar salads. They are spicy snacks for late at night or even as a pick-me-up. I never figured out why flavored croutons never made it big time into the retail snack market. To me, they are almost the perfect snack, especially when you make them yourself without any preservatives.

1 cup cubed bread
1 tablespoon olive oil
1 teaspoon garlic powder

½ teaspoon dried oregano
½ teaspoon dried basil
¼ cup shredded or grated Parmesan cheese
    (optional)
Sprinkle of dried parsley (optional)

Prepare the croutons according to the directions for Cheesy Soup Croutons (page 144). For this recipe, allow more time for the Italian spices to impart flavor to the croutons before blending in the cheese.

Quick Chicken Liver Pâté

Remember that great scene in *The Godfather: Part II* when Frankie "Five Fingers" is at Michael Corleone's party in Nevada and remarks at how times have changed. He's eating pâté on a cracker, but says that he's really eating chopped liver.

For movie critics writing about how movies depict social history in America, this was a telling scene. But for most of us, it was more about what would eventually happen to Frankie "Five Fingers." No matter what your take is on the movie, you can enjoy this recipe at home anytime: at parties, as an appetizer, or, you guessed it, late at night. A pretty crock of pâté is an especially welcome addition to any gift basket.

½ cup (1 stick) butter, at room temperature
½ cup Homemade Cream Cheese (page 44), at
    room temperature
1 pound chicken livers
1 cup water

1 small onion, quartered

2 garlic cloves, minced

4 cubes (2 ounces) chicken bouillon

1 teaspoon dried thyme

1 teaspoon paprika

1 teaspoon dried tarragon

½ teaspoon cayenne pepper

¼ teaspoon ground allspice

¼ teaspoon ground cloves

2 tablespoons brandy

1. Carefully rinse the chicken livers, cut in half, and remove any connective tissue. Place the chicken livers in a saucepan with the water, onion, garlic, and bouillon cubes. Bring to a boil, cover, and simmer for 20 minutes, or until the livers and onion are tender.

2. Place the livers, onion, garlic, 2 tablespoons of the boiling liquid, and herbs and spices in the jar of a blender or bowl of a food processor and blend for 1 minute. Add the butter and cream cheese and blend for 1 minute more. Scrape down the jar or bowl, add the brandy, and blend until the mixture is smooth.

3. Pour the pâté into a small crock or serving dish, cover with plastic wrap, and refrigerate for 2 hours. Set the pâté out at room temperature for 15 minutes before serving. The pâté will keep in the refrigerator for 2 weeks if covered tightly.

Makes 24 ounces pâté

Turkey Pesto

Let's say you really want to prepare a quick summer sandwich or a spicy, deep winter turkey main course with an Italian flavor. You can use the same recipe, heated or chilled, either way.

My suggestion is that unless you are a serious Italian cooking maven, buy your pesto sauce in your supermarket. However, you can add a fresh touch by either garnishing your dish with fresh basil or even adding some to the recipe at the end, along with parsley and a little bit of oregano.

> 3 cups cubed, cooked leftover turkey or white
>   meat chicken
> One 16-ounce container store-bought pesto
>   sauce
> 1 sweet bell pepper, seeded and very finely
>   chopped
> 1 hot pepper, seeded and very finely chopped
>   (optional)
> 1 small onion, finely chopped
> 1 large fresh basil leaf, chopped (optional)
> ¼ cup grated Parmesan or Pecorino Romano
>   cheese

1. In a small saucepan over low heat, bring the pesto just to a simmer.

2. While the pesto is heating, combine the turkey or chicken, bell pepper, hot pepper, if using, onion, and fresh basil in a bowl.

3. Add the turkey to the pesto and stir in the grated cheese. Transfer to a serving dish and serve on its own, or use as a topping over heated Italian or garlic bread, or even on a slice of panini or ciabatta.

Makes 3 cups pesto

Curried Turkey or Chicken Sloppy Joes

This is a very easy recipe, spicy, to be sure, but also sweet and tart because you add cubed green Granny Smith apples along with spicy red pepper. As with many of these recipes, make this up in advance so that when you have a midnight craving, just heat up the curried sloppy Joes, find yourself a nice pita pocket or hamburger bun, and enjoy.

You've probably guessed by now that I am a big fan of cumin seed in Latin, Middle Eastern, and Indian dishes.

> 2 cups cubed, cooked turkey or white meat chicken
> 1 Granny Smith apple, peeled, finely chopped
> 1 small onion (Vidalia, if available)
> 3 fresh celery stalks, minced
> 2 small ripe tomatoes or plum tomatoes
> 1 cup Cilantro Mayonnaise (page 153) or Mustard Mayonnaise (page 284), or plain mayo if that suits your taste
> 2 teaspoons curry powder (see page 67)
> 1 teaspoon ground cumin or whole cumin seeds
> Salt and freshly ground black pepper

1. Combine the apples, onions, celery, and tomatoes in a large bowl.

2. Heat up the cubed, cooked turkey or chicken in a microwave for 2 minutes.

3. Add the warm turkey or chicken to the apples, onions, celery, and tomatoes in the bowl and combine thoroughly.

4. Add the mayonnaise and stir through until the ingredients are coated and bound together in a chunky mix.

5. Slowly add the curry powder to taste, and the cumin, salt, and pepper, one by one, and stir through for each spice.

6. Cover the bowl and let sit for 15 to 20 minutes to let the curry powder percolate through the ingredients.

7. At this point, you can taste to see if there is enough bite or if you want to add more curry or cumin seed. Season with more salt and pepper to taste.

8. Serve the sloppy Joes in pita pockets, whole wheat or white, with bean sprouts. Or spoon over whole wheat or white hamburger buns. For another variation, serve on good, old-fashioned Pennsylvania Dutch potato rolls or bagels topped with sliced tomato and even sliced onion.

Makes 3 to 4 servings

Gingerbread Puzzles

I remember one of the greatest things about the winter holiday season was gingerbread cookies and pastries. You can still get them, of course, especially the ones imported from England. But if you make them yourself, you always have them on hand, can prepare lots of different variations, especially icing them up with a nice imported lemon curd, and enjoy them in the middle of the night with a cup of strong tea. Here is one of my favorite gingerbread recipes made from scratch.

This batter can become the basis for a castle or a gingerbread man or woman, but a holiday puzzle that children can actually play with before eating is a nice idea if you're making the gingerbread for a special small person. Follow a simple puzzle design from a child's set or invent a simple one to suit the occasion or the interests of the child.

DOUGH
½ cup light molasses
½ cup (1 stick) butter or margarine
½ cup sugar
1 large egg, lightly beaten
1 teaspoon baking soda
1 teaspoon ground cinnamon
1 teaspoon ground cloves
1 teaspoon ground ginger
2¾ cups all-purpose flour

FROSTING
2 tablespoons Homemade Cream Cheese (page 44)
½ cup Powdered Vanilla Sugar (page 180)
1 tablespoon whole milk
1 teaspoon finely grated orange zest

DECORATION
Silly Sparkles (page 276)

1. In a medium saucepan, bring the molasses to a boil. Remove from the heat and add the butter and sugar. Set aside to cool.
2. Stir in the egg, baking soda, spices, and flour, ½ cup at a time. Wrap the dough in plastic wrap or aluminum foil and refrigerate overnight or for at least 8 hours.

3. Preheat the oven to 350°F. Grease two baking sheets.

4. Remove the dough from the refrigerator and let it soften for 15 minutes. Roll out the dough on a lightly floured surface. Divide the dough in half and roll out each half into a thickness of ⅛ inch. Cut into two 12 by 9-inch rectangles and place on the prepared baking sheets.

5. Bake for 10 minutes. Remove from the oven, leave the gingerbread on the baking sheets, and cut your design out with a sharp paring knife. You can place an outline cut from paper for the main figure in the middle to guide you, or you can cut the design out freehand. Cut the remainder of the rectangles to resemble puzzle pieces. Do not lift any of the pieces up, but make sure you've cut all the way through the dough. Return the baking sheets with the gingerbread to the oven and continue to bake for another 5 minutes, or until set. Test the gingerbread by inserting a toothpick in the thickest part; the toothpick will come out clean when the gingerbread is set.

6. Cool for 5 minutes on the baking pan, and then carefully transfer to a wire rack and let cool completely.

7. To make the frosting, stir the milk into the cream cheese and add the sugar slowly, stirring briskly to blend. Stir in the grated orange zest. The frosting will be thin. If you would like a thicker frosting, add a bit more sugar.

8. Cut the corner off a clean envelope to make a funnel for the Silly Sparkles. Frost the cookies and before the frosting is completely dry, sprinkle the puzzle pieces with the silly sugar.

Makes two 12 by 9-inch cookies

Cilantro Mayonnaise

This is an especially delicate mayonnaise, which combines both cilantro and oregano. It is a very utilitarian sandwich spread, and a wonderful spice-it-up for chicken as well as turkey sandwiches or even roast beef or cold pot roast for that matter.

½ cup regular mayonnaise or light mayonnaise
2 tablespoons finely chopped or ground fresh
    cilantro
1 teaspoon Worcestershire sauce
1 to 2 drops Tabasco or your favorite hot sauce
2 drops lemon juice
Salt and freshly ground black pepper

Combine all of the ingredients until thoroughly blended.

Makes ½ cup mayonnaise

Schmageggies

Who needs a fast-food restaurant, eggs whatever, when you can make these yourself, fast and easy and fresh. Schmageggies are my absolutely favorite quick treat when I need a morning pick-me-up after I get back from the studio, even if it's only going upstairs from my cave studio in St. Louis.

What's a schmageggie? I always think of it as a strange-looking creature out of an Al Capp cartoon. Actually, a schmageggie is a wonderful egg-on-a-bun treat where the variety is in

Schmageggies

VARIATIONS:

the type of bun you use—try Pennsylvania Dutch potato roll buns—or in the type of cheese you melt on top. Of course, the basic cheese is good old American cheese slices. But, as tangy as American cheese is, think of a slice of Muenster, Swiss, a mild cheddar, or, let's misbehave and try a slice of provolone.

> **2 hamburger buns, white or whole wheat or**
> **   potato roll buns**
> **2 tablespoons butter, or 2 pats of butter**
> **2 large eggs**
> **1 to 2 slices American cheese**
> **Pinch of salt**
> **Pinch of freshly ground black pepper**
> **Pinch of paprika (optional)**
> **Celery salt or seed (optional)**

1. Scoop out the center of the bottom buns, but don't let the hole go all the way through to the bottom.
2. Soften the butter in your microwave first and then place a bit of butter in the hole in the bottom of the bun. Carefully break an egg into the hole of each bun and season with pinches of salt, pepper, paprika, and/or celery salt or seed.
3. Microwave on medium-high for 4 minutes, then check for doneness. Microwave another 2 minutes, or as needed, on high until the eggs are done. Making sure the eggs are done is important because, unless you're Rocky, you do not want to eat raw-ish eggs.
4. When the eggs are done, top each bun with a slice or half slice of cheese, and microwave for another 60 seconds or until the cheese melts. Add the top halves of the buns and heat for another 10 seconds, let the schmageggies sit for 5 seconds, and serve.

Makes 2 schmageggies

VARIATIONS   You can vary the type of bun or roll, vary the type and flavor of cheese, vary the seasonings, pump up the heat level by sprinkling on hot sauce, or even dumping the yolks and cooking egg white schmageggies. These things also hold up well to wrapping them up individually after they're cooked, refrigerating them, and then reheating them later.

This is like having a fast-food restaurant in your own kitchen, and I haven't even mentioned what you can do with sausage patties or veggie sausage on top of the egg and cheese. Want a great breakfast fast? Try my schmageggies.

7

• NATURE • ENVIRONMENT • • EARTH CHANGES •

Well, you know what this chapter is going to be about. I don't think I've heard so many prepper ideas and interviews, well, ever. If you're reading this, of course the earth didn't disintegrate in 2012, so you just might have a few extra tins of emergency supplies to think about.

After all, they won't last forever, so it's best to rotate your stock, eat a little now, save a little for the future. Was the future ever certain? It's great to be prepared, and there are some fine tips to be had here.

It's never a bad idea to prepare for a rainy day, a power outage, a big snowstorm that banks your doorway. Or worse. So, learn to cure and store your own food for long-term planning and most important, learn how to cook with those carefully stored and precious ingredients.

The Microwave Drying Process

Let's start with microwave drying. Don't limit yourself to just veggies. You can dry the peels from oranges, lemons, and limes, coat them with sweetener or sugar, and portion them to kids as dessert snacks in their lunches. Enjoy them yourself as snacks and little hits of sugar at night to keep you going at work. If this seems like a harsh candy recipe, fine, you can use these dried, but not scorched rinds to flavor drinks or for pure decoration. A dish of these dried fruit peels, maybe sprinkled with ground cinnamon, will also make a potpourri and, if you can sew or find someone who can, a filling for a nice bouquet-filled head cushion. Just think what your microwave is capable of creating.

Microwave Sun-Dried Tomatoes

Perfect on olive oil–drenched toast, your homemade English muffin pizzas, any pasta dish, or any sandwich, these microwave sun-dried tomatoes are also easy to make and a perfect garnish or complement to any dish. If you've ever had sun-dried tomatoes at your neighborhood cucina or your favorite Italian restaurant, you know how good they can be. Try them with melted fresh mozzarella cheese and basil. And if you use them with the best first-pressed, extra-virgin olive oil you can afford, this recipe will reward you with much pleasure.

Sun-dried tomatoes are a gourmet item that you can make up right in your own microwave oven. However, because tomatoes must be dried carefully, you will have to keep an eye on them during the entire drying process. Remember, microwave drying is a lot more potent than sun-drying. Therefore, it's easy to overcook and scorch the food you're drying.

However, in many places in the U.S., sun-drying is just not possible because the climate is not hot enough for a sustained period of time to let the sun do its work. Therefore, microwave drying, especially in the northern U.S., is probably the most efficient method of sun-drying your tomatoes.

> 3 pounds ripe plum tomatoes
> 2 teaspoons salt
> 1½ cups extra-virgin olive oil, preferably first
>   pressed
> garlic (optional)
> hot peppers (optional)
> fresh basil (optional)

1. Rinse the tomatoes in warm water, and then pat dry with paper towels.
2. Cut the tomatoes lengthwise.
3. Place the tomatoes, cut side up, on a microwave rack over paper towels on a microwave-safe dish.
4. Sprinkle with salt.
5. Dry in 15-minute cycles on the lowest microwave setting, rotating the tray between cycles if your microwave does not automatically rotate. Test both for dryness and firmness between the 15-minute cycles, whether or not you need to rotate.
6. Continue drying in cycles for 3 hours, or until the tomatoes are flexible but not moist. You may have to adjust the drying cycles depending on how much you can adjust the power of your microwave. After the drying process is complete, set aside the tomatoes and cool completely.

Microwave Sun-Dried Tomatoes

7. Pack the newly dried tomatoes in a sterilized glass jar, cover with olive oil, and store in a cool, dry place before serving. You can also flavor the olive oil you're using to drench the tomatoes by infusing it with crushed fresh garlic cloves, chopped hot peppers, or even a ¼ teaspoon of basil.

8. Store the tomatoes in oil for at least a month before serving. You may also ask why it's important that your glass container be sterile, and how to do that. You sterilize it by slowly heating it in water and slowly letting it cool, lest the glass shatter. Microwave-safe glass containers can be heated in the microwave and allowed to cool before use. We sterilize the container because tomatoes themselves are very friendly to certain bacteria that can make you sick. Therefore, when canning tomatoes with any recipe, you should be careful about the container you're storing them in.

Makes 16 ounces sun-dried tomatoes

Indeed, this is a project, a slow process, but if done when you have time and the dried tomatoes are stored properly, it will be well worth the time spent to create this late-night treat.

Dried Veggies for the Long Haul

Here is a handy way to use up celery before it becomes all limp and uncouth in the refrigerator, or to store away a nice harvest of peppers. I always buy celery, scallions, and carrots with the best of intentions, but whenever I need some in a recipe, they are usually too far gone to slice.

Drying a batch of vegetables is an easy way to keep them chopped and handy when you need them. Freezing chopped, uncooked vegetables is another way to store them for cooking, and if you use them without thawing, the vegetables will re-constitute rather well.

> 1 to 2 cups vegetables, finely chopped: onions, mushrooms, red or green bell peppers, scallions, or celery

1. Preheat the oven to 120°F.
2. Spread the finely chopped vegetables in a thin layer on a baking sheet. Dry in the oven until crisp. The drying time will vary, depending on the amount of moisture in the air and in the vegetables. Plan on leaving the baking sheet in the oven for at least 12 hours, stirring occasionally.
3. Cool and store the veggies immediately in a sterilized, dry glass or metal container with a tight-fitting lid. The veggies will keep for up to 6 months in the pantry.

Makes 2 cups dried veggies

HINT   If you want to conserve energy, try drying the vegetables in the sun. Pick a dry, sunny day and place the baking sheet in full sunlight. Cover loosely with cheesecloth or arrange a screen over the sheet. The trick is to ensure air circulation and the drying effect of the sun, and at the same time to protect the vegetables from insects and critters. Take the sheet in at night and repeat the drying process for 1 to 3 days, or until the vegetables are thoroughly dried.

If you use the sun-drying method, place the food in the oven at 125°F for 1 hour, or store the food in the freezer for 24 hours before using to kill any insect eggs, which may be invisible, but there.

Corn on the Job

To dry corn, husk and clean ears of corn and then steam or blanch for 3 minutes. Drain, cut the kernels off the cobs, and dry using the same method as for Dried Veggies (see page 162). When fully dry, the corn should be hard and brittle.

TO USE   Pour 2 cups boiling water over 1 cup dry corn and simmer, covered, for 1 hour.

Dried Tomatoes in Oil

Just like the marinated mushroom dish, you can enjoy dried tomatoes in oil at any time for any meal or snack. You can also fold them into an omelet or scrambled eggs, on toast at breakfast, or as a late-night, radio-listening snack.

These tomatoes are very expensive in gourmet shops, and once you taste them, you'll want to make your own to use with abandon. They are perfect served with very fresh, creamy mozzarella cheese and garnished with fresh basil. Use the very best olive oil you can afford for this recipe and save the oil and use it to make delicious salads.

Since the tomatoes must be slowly and carefully dried, it's a good idea to place a thermometer in your oven so that you can maintain an even temperature of 150°F. It is not recommended that you try sun-drying your tomatoes because our summers are neither hot nor long enough to do the job as slowly and thoroughly as necessary.

3 pounds ripe plum tomatoes
2 teaspoons salt
1½ cups olive oil

1. Preheat the oven to 150°F.
2. Rinse the tomatoes in warm water and pat dry. Cut lengthwise and place, cut side up, on a wire rack set over a baking sheet. Sprinkle with salt.
3. Place the racks of tomatoes in the oven and leave the door ajar, about 4 inches. Check the temperature every 2 hours and rotate the pans to ensure even drying. Turn off the oven for 30 minutes if the temperature rises over 150°F. Dry for 12 hours, or until the tomatoes are flexible but not moist. Set aside to cool.
4. Pack the dried tomatoes in a sterilized glass jar, cover with olive oil, and store in a cool, dry place for 1 month before using.

Makes 16 ounces tomatoes in oil

Fruit Leathers

Many people might not remember this type of fruit candy, but I do. It was the type of candy, also called "shoe leather," that you could take to school in your lunch box, start chewing it on the bus, and still have enough for lunch and for the bus ride home. That was then.

Now, in the green millennium, this delicious way to preserve, store, and eat fruit has just recently come back into fashion. Fruit leathers are fun to pull at and to eat, and they are full of flavor. Their light weight and long chewability make them ideal to pack for hiking and for school lunches. To get the best flavors, it's a good idea to use fruit when it is at a very ripe stage.

> **2 cups very ripe fruit: fresh, frozen, cooked, or**
> **canned**
> **½ cup sugar or honey**

1. Pour the fruit and sweetener into the jar of a blender and puree until you have a very fine pulp.
2. Line a baking sheet with plastic wrap and tape the edges securely with masking tape. Pour the puree over the plastic wrap, spreading it with a spatula so that it is a uniform thickness of about ⅛ inch.
3. Dry the puree by one of the methods below until the puree is dry on the surface, but still pliable.

   There are several methods for drying fruit: in the sun, in the oven, with a commercial dehydrator, or with a convection oven. You can even try using your microwave, but each model has different controls and different wattages, so the results are not entirely predictable.

   To dry in the sun, make sure you've chosen a day with plenty of sun and low humidity. You will need 2 to 3 days of full sun, and you must bring your sheet in at night. Cover the baking sheet with cheesecloth to keep insects away from the fruit. When the fruit is dry, place it in a 120°F oven for 1 hour before cooling and storing.

   If you decide to use a conventional oven, set the temperature at 150°F and dry the fruit for 6 to 12 hours, depending on the type of fruit. To be safe, leave the oven door ajar to check on the fruit, and rotate the sheet every 2 hours.
4. Remove the fruit leather from the baking sheet, leaving the plastic wrap as a backing. Cut the fruit leather into narrow

strips and roll it up. Store the rolls in an airtight container for up to 8 weeks.

Makes 16 ounces fruit leather

NOTE   A crushed vitamin C tablet will provide enough ascorbic acid in a peach or pear mixture to keep the fruit from browning.

VARIATIONS   You can add a tablespoon of lemon juice to flavor some of the fruit puree, if you wish, and you can sprinkle the puree spread out in the pan with chopped nuts.

For raw apple leather, add ½ cup apple cider and ¼ teaspoon ground cinnamon to 2 cups peeled and cored apples.

Noodle Mix to Order

Like mac and cheese? Like Italian-style or Southwestern mac and cheese, or even noodles and cheese? How about using different shapes, such as wagon wheels, for a kids' hot lunch. You can buy packaged noodles and cheese mixes, of course, but for real variety, freshness, savings, and environmental friendliness, try this very easy recipe and you will always have a great mix for your midnight macaroni or other favorite pasta shape.

>   1 cup instant nonfat dry milk
>   2 tablespoons finely grated Parmesan or
>   Pecorino Romano cheese
>   ⅓ cup onion, minced (Here is also where you can
>   use your dried onion pieces or your freeze-
>   dried onion.)

1 tablespoon garlic powder
½ teaspoon salt
½ teaspoon ground white pepper

1. Combine all of the above ingredients in a microwave-safe dish. Microwave on high power for 1 minute.
2. Remove from the microwave to check for dryness, and then microwave for 1 minute more on high, if the mixture is not completely dry.
3. Store in a tightly closed container in your pantry where it will keep for up to 4 months.

TO USE   To make your Parmesan mac and cheese, combine ¼ cup of your mix with 2 tablespoons melted butter and ¼ cup whole milk. Melt the butter in the microwave, where you can also warm the milk, and toss the sauce through your favorite pasta: elbow macaroni, small shells, or any shape you like.

Makes 1 to 2 cups noodle mix

VARIATIONS
◆ **New England–Style Mac and Cheese:** If you replace the Parmesan or Pecorino Romano with medium to sharp cheddar cheese, toss over elbow macaroni in a microwave-safe dish, and then top with croutons, you will have a hearty, old-fashioned macaroni and cheddar casserole.
◆ **Instant Pasta Primavera:** For a main-dish casserole, try stirring cooked baby peas or snow peas, pine nuts (pignoli), and carrot slivers through the pasta before you blend in the cheese mixture. A milder cheese will bring out the flavors of the instant pasta primavera you have just created. Everything depends on the pasta shape you choose.

◆ **Southwestern Mac and Cheese:** For a Southwestern-style pasta, use a combination of cheddar and Jack cheeses, grated and mixed together. You can replace the macaroni with the same amount of rice or couscous for a different variation on an old favorite.

If I could, I would have a bowl of any variation of this recipe in my studio every night. However, the sound of my slurping would be very disturbing to the listening audience so I have to wait until I get home after the show to indulge.

Raisin Sauce

Got ham? Ever try smoked tongue? Maybe just spread a little of this on some white or whole wheat toast or a Wheat Thin. It's great.

Try this sauce brushed on a nice Sunday ham before you place it in the oven. Baste the ham with the juices and baste with additional sauce as the ham bakes. You can add any sort of fruit as a garnish near the end of the cooking time: peaches, pineapple, or more raisins and grapes.

Also, cold ham with raisin sauce on rye or pumpernickel makes an amazing sandwich in the middle of the night when you get up to listen to one of my guests on *Coast*.

½ cup packed brown sugar
1 tablespoon all-purpose flour
1 tablespoon Tangy Mustard (page 201)
1½ cups water
½ cup cider vinegar
½ cup raisins

Mix all of the ingredients in a saucepan and simmer for 10 minutes. Store the sauce in a sterilized glass jar in the refrigerator. The sauce will keep for 2 to 4 months.

TO USE   Use this sauce as a glaze over poultry as well as ham. The glaze is best brushed on as you begin to roast, and then refreshed during the roasting process.

You can make a delicious gravy by thickening the juices that are flavored with the Raisin Sauce.

Makes 16 ounces sauce

Happy Trails Mix

For an even lighter snack, available right by the radio or computer any time night or day, but especially night, try these trail mix snacks. Store individual servings of this snack in plastic sandwich bags and pack one with your lunch or in a camper's backpack for a healthy, high-energy alternative to a candy bar. See Healthy Seed Treats (page 45) for how to prepare your own seeds for this mixture.

> 1 cup sunflower seeds
> 1 cup almonds
> 1 cup hazelnuts
> 1 cup raisins
> ½ cup shredded unsweetened coconut
> 2 cups various dried fruits: bananas, pineapple,
>   apricots, apples

In a large bowl, mix together all of the ingredients. Store the mixture in an airtight container, or make up individual snack packs in plastic bags and store the individual packs in the airtight container. The snack mix will keep for 2 to 4 months on the pantry shelf.

Makes 6 cups (48 ounces) trail mix

8

• PROPHECY • PREDICTIONS •
• SPIRITUALITY • OCCULT •

Betty's Insta-Sweets

Basic Chocolate Sauce

Hot Fudge Sauce

Scented and Spiced Sugars

Powdered Vanilla Sugar

Cinnamon-Sugar

Pudding Mixes

Garlic Butter

French Herb Butter

Country "Butter"

Ooh-la-la Butter

Homemade Peanut Butter

*Spicy Lemon Salt
Substitute*

Sesame Seasoning Salt

*Great Seasonings Salad
Dressing Mix*

Mexican Seasoning Mix

*Firehouse Hot Chili
Powder*

Tangy Mustard

Sweet Berry Syrups

*Sweetened
Condensed Milk*

Vanilla Bean Extract

*Polka-Dotties:
The Glynnis McCann
Special*

Predictions, no matter how dire, at least suggest a viable future for us. So, even though the shows can be worrying at times, it's important to keep a sense of humor in the face of ultimate knowledge of coming events.

Here in this chapter I've assembled a whole lot of recipes to help you stock your pantry so that you will always have something to eat in the future.

If you think that your handy microwave is just for heating up late-morning, leftover coffee or those pizza slices from the night before, think again. You can make lots of happy snack-like foods in your microwave, which is why I see it as the magic appliance for *Coast to Coast* fans. Lots of talk show hosts, I have heard from those who know, have microwave ovens in their studios for quick snacks during station breaks and news feeds.

I have two studios: one in California and one in my home outside St. Louis, which I call "the cave." I like to have a microwave nearby so I can bring my ready-to-nuke snacks and enjoy them, nice and hot, when I am ready to eat.

Also, a microwave is the perfect late-night appliance. Not only does it keep time—if you set it right and adjust it twice a year when the time changes—but it is that friendly set of digits that can even give you messages like 9:11, 4:11, and, my favorites, 7:11 and 11:07.

Listen to the show and let the numerical experts guide you, and you can decide what these messages mean for you.

Betty's Insta-Sweets

These treats are the particular favorites of Betty in Richmond Heights, Missouri.

Ever want a perfect cookie in the middle of the night? When you work all night, as I do, it's almost part of the job. I figured out a solution you will like, too.

This is a treat made mostly from store-bought items that you can make quickly in large batches and save for whenever you want them. You can express your own creativity with this treat, and your children can, too. But the best thing about this is that it will satisfy your urge for cookies by keeping the cookie-monster seed in you at bay.

Just make sure you have all of the required ingredients on hand so that you can make these up at any time. I promise you that neither you nor the junior bakers who assist you will run out of creative ideas for these cookies.

> 1 or more packages store-bought cookies, basic
>   sugar cookies, or shortbread cookies
> ½ cup each of the following:
>   • Honey
>   • Butter
>   • Crunchy peanut butter
>   • Chocolate bars
>   • Chocolate kisses
>   • Shredded coconut

1. Arrange the cookies on a flat microwave-safe sheet. In a bowl, combine honey, butter, and peanut butter.
2. Soften the mixture by microwaving it on the lowest setting for 1½ minutes. Spoon the honey-butter mixture onto the

individual cookies and set the chocolate bars, chocolate kisses, and coconut on top, in any configuration that strikes your fancy.

Makes as many cookies as you want

You can store these cookies in the refrigerator, wrap them up individually and put them in your child's lunch box, or take them to work with you. I like the idea, however, that when I have a yen for a late-night treat, I can make them up in under 5 minutes and eat them, nice and warm, with milk, tea, or hot chocolate.

Basic Chocolate Sauce

This tasty sauce can be varied in hundreds of ways, depending on your audience and on the fancy ingredients you have on hand. Soon you will have developed your own chocolate specialties, and why not package your special sauce in small, pretty jars and give them as gifts? It's always good to share!

> 2 ounces semisweet baking chocolate
> 2 tablespoons butter
> ½ cup boiling water
> 1½ cups sugar
> Dash of salt
> 1 teaspoon Vanilla Bean Extract (page 205)

1. Melt the chocolate in an enamel double boiler or in a glass bowl set over a saucepan of simmering water.

2. Stir in the butter, then boiling water, then the sugar and salt. Cook, stirring occasionally, for 15 minutes.

3. Remove from the heat and stir in the vanilla.

4. This sauce is best when served warm. Use immediately, or reheat in a double boiler for 10 minutes or in a microwave for 1 minute on high.

5. To store the sauce, pour it into sterilized glass jars. Allow the sauce to cool, then refrigerate. The sauce will keep for 6 months.

Makes ½ cup sauce, more or less

VARIATIONS   Add any of the following flavorings in place of or in addition to the vanilla in step 3:

- 1 teaspoon orange extract or ⅓ cup orange juice
- 1 teaspoon mint extract
- ⅛ cup crushed strawberries or raspberries, chopped raisins or nuts
- 1 tablespoon crème de menthe, coffee liqueur, spicy orange cordial, or Grand Marnier
- 1 teaspoon instant coffee

Hot Fudge Sauce

A richer, smoother sauce—this enduring classic melts in the mouth. Make extra!

1 cup Sweetened Condensed Milk (page 204)
1 cup sugar
¼ cup light corn syrup

4 tablespoons (½ stick) butter
5 ounces semisweet baking chocolate
1 teaspoon Vanilla Bean Extract (page 205)

1. Combine all of the ingredients in the top of a double boiler or in a glass bowl set over a saucepan of simmering water. Cook over low heat, stirring constantly, until the mixture is smooth and all the chocolate is melted.
2. Cool the sauce and store it in a sterilized glass jar in the refrigerator for up to 4 weeks. Let it warm to room temperature before using.

Makes 16 ounces fudge sauce

Scented and Spiced Sugars

These delicately colored and lightly scented sugars are an excellent accompaniment to Unadulterated Adult Herbal Teas (page 62), and are delicious sprinkled on buttered toast or pancakes in the morning. Also try these sugars to flavor fresh fruit, especially bananas, and to top off applesauce or sliced peaches. For the strongest taste, use freshly grated citrus peel and freshly ground spices, if you have a spice grinder.

Citrus and Spice Sugar

1 cup sugar
1 tablespoon finely grated orange zest
1 teaspoon finely grated lemon zest
½ teaspoon ground cinnamon
¼ teaspoon ground nutmeg
¼ teaspoon ground ginger

1. Preheat the oven to 200°F.
2. Mix all of the ingredients in a shallow baking pan. Bake in the oven for 15 minutes, stirring occasionally. Set aside to cool.
3. Pour the mixture into a blender and whirl on low speed until the ingredients are blended and the sugar is finely ground. Stored in a tightly closed container, the sugar will keep for up to 6 months.

Lemon and Mint Sugar

> 1 cup sugar
> 1 tablespoon dried mint leaves or 4 to 5 fresh mint leaves, or try anise, lemon verbena, or rose-geranium leaves for variation
> 1 tablespoon finely grated lemon zest

1. Preheat the oven to 200°F.
2. Mix all of the ingredients in a shallow baking pan. Bake in the oven for 15 minutes, stirring occasionally. If you are using fresh mint, bake for an additional 10 minutes, or until the leaves are crunchy. Set aside to cool.
3. Pour the mixture into a blender and whirl on low speed until the ingredients are well blended and the sugar is finely ground. Stored in a tightly closed container, the sugar will keep for up to 6 months.

Rose Sugar

> Petals of 1 fragrant, pesticide-free rose
> 1 cup sugar

1. Wash the rose petals thoroughly, making sure that any soil

is completely rinsed off. If you are using pesticide-free rose petals from your garden, you also want to check for any little insects or aphids that are making a home there. Dry the rose petals.

2. Pour the sugar into a clean glass jar with a tight-fitting lid. Bury the rose in the sugar and place the jar in full sunlight. Shake the jar every other day for 2 to 3 weeks.

TO USE   You can use this sugar in place of regular sugar in many recipes—the sugar will seem a bit sweeter.

This sugar is delightful sprinkled on fresh or brandied fruit, or served with one of the Unadulterated Adult Herbal Teas (page 62).

Dust through a fancy doily onto freshly made chocolate or pound cake, or try some in Spiced and Fancy After-Dinner Coffee (page 223).

Each recipe makes about 9 ounces scented and spiced sugar

VARIATION   If you would like to try a rose-flavored powdered vanilla sugar, simply place 1 cup of flavored sugar, without the beans or blossoms, into your blender with 1 teaspoon cornstarch and blend on high speed for 2 minutes, or until the sugar is a fine powder. Let the mixture rest for a week or two before using to make sure the cornstarch flavor is absorbed.

Powdered Vanilla Sugar

I'll bet you didn't know that powdered, or confectioners', sugar is just regular sugar put through a blender at high speed, did you? This is especially handy to know if you think you've run out of powdered sugar and therefore you can't ice your cupcakes. Never fear: just ask yourself, Will it blend? It will.

To make this recipe a little more economical, you might consider using the expensive vanilla beans first to make Vanilla Bean Extract (page 205), and then after a few weeks, remove them from the extract and add them to the sugar. Then you will have two lovely vanilla-flavored items in your kitchen pantry for the price of the vanilla beans.

> **2 cups granulated sugar**
> **2 vanilla beans**

1. Place the sugar in an airtight canister or jar with a tight-fitting lid. Using kitchen shears or sturdy scissors, cut the vanilla bean into 3 or 4 pieces, working directly over the jar or container so that all of the little black seeds will drop into the sugar.
2. Cover and store for 2 to 4 weeks before using. If you have lumps in the sugar, remove the beans and whirl in the blender for 1 minute. Additional plain sugar may be added to the container as you use your vanilla sugar until you notice that the scent and flavor are gone.

Makes 16 ounces powdered vanilla sugar

Cinnamon-Sugar

This particular pantry stocker is considered a necessity in certain families. People tell me they feel safe and secure knowing it is in the closet, and they love to sprinkle it on hot buttered toast or English muffins. You can smell the heavenly aroma the minute it's sprinkled on, so be liberal with it.

2 cups sugar
⅓ cup ground cinnamon

Stir the sugar and cinnamon together until completely mixed. Store in a clean spice jar with a shaker top for up to 6 months.

TO USE   Shake this mixture over just about any food when your sweet tooth acts up: oatmeal, buttered toast, dusted over whipped cream, in coffee—these are just for starters.

Try it also in tea; for French toast, see Ooh-la-la Butter, page 192; on puddings, see the recipe below; any of the ice cream recipes you can make yourself; on yogurt, see page 42; over jelly; and dusted over any fruit pie, especially pumpkin.

Makes 20 ounces cinnamon-sugar

VARIATIONS   Reduce the ground cinnamon by 1 tablespoon and add 1 tablespoon ground allspice or 1 tablespoon ground nutmeg. For more exotic mixes, see Scented and Spiced Sugars (page 178). For a colorful mix for parties or holidays, see Silly Sparkles (page 276). For a silky taste, try Powdered Vanilla Sugar (page 180).

Pudding Mixes

The basic mix will make twenty batches of pudding, divided into 4½-cup servings of each. Below are instructions for making a basic pudding from the mix, as well as some suggestions for fancier, richer puddings.

Vanilla Pudding Mix

> 3 cups instant nonfat dry milk
> 4 cups sugar
> 1 teaspoon salt
> 3 cups cornstarch
> 1 vanilla bean

1. Mix together the milk, sugar, salt, and cornstarch until the ingredients are well blended.

2. Cut the vanilla bean into several large pieces and stir them into the mix, seeds and all. Store the mix in an airtight container or a jar with a tight-fitting lid.

TO USE   Stir the mix in the container, then measure out ½ cup and add to a saucepan. Add 2 cups whole milk and cook over low heat, stirring, until the mixture comes to a boil and thickens.

Continue stirring for 1 minute, remove from the heat, and pour into individual serving dishes. The pudding will thicken further as it cools.

Makes 32 ounces of pudding

VARIATION   For a richer-tasting pudding, try cooking as directed and after taking the pudding off the heat, stir in an egg, lightly beaten with ½ teaspoon ground nutmeg, ½ teaspoon Vanilla Bean Extract (page 205), and 1 tablespoon unsalted butter. Cover and let sit for a minute or two. Uncover and stir, then pour into individual serving dishes.

Chocolate Pudding Mix

2½ cups instant nonfat dry milk
5 cups sugar
3 cups cornstarch
1 teaspoon salt
2½ cups unsweetened cocoa powder

Mix all of the ingredients until they are well blended. Store the mix in an airtight container or a jar with a tight-fitting lid.

TO USE   Stir the mix in the container, then measure out ⅔ cup and add to a saucepan. Add 2 cups whole milk and cook over low heat, stirring, until the mixture comes to a boil and thickens.

Continue stirring for 1 minute, remove from the heat, and pour into individual serving dishes. The pudding will thicken further as it cools.

Makes 32 ounces of pudding

VARIATION   Cook as directed, but add 1 teaspoon Vanilla Bean Extract (page 205) and 1 tablespoon unsalted butter to the pudding as it cooks.

For a chocolate-mocha flavor, add 1 tablespoon instant coffee to the pudding mix before cooking.

Butterscotch Pudding Mix

2 cups instant nonfat dry milk
5 cups firmly packed brown sugar

3 cups cornstarch
1 teaspoon salt

Mix all of the ingredients until they are well blended. Store the mix in an airtight container or a jar with a tight-fitting lid.

TO USE   Stir the mix in the container, then measure out ½ cup and add to a saucepan. Add 2 cups whole milk and 4 table-spoons (½ stick) butter and cook over low heat, stirring, until the mixture comes to a boil and thickens. Continue stirring for 1 minute, remove from the heat, and pour into individual serving dishes. The pudding will thicken further as it cools.

Makes 32 ounces of pudding

VARIATION   Add ½ cup chopped peanuts to the pudding when you take it off the heat.

Coconut Cream Pudding Mix

3 cups instant nonfat dry milk
4 cups sugar
1 teaspoon salt
3 cups cornstarch
1½ cups shredded, unsweetened coconut
1 teaspoon coconut extract

1. Mix the milk, sugar, salt, and cornstarch together until the ingredients are well blended.
2. Whirl the coconut and the coconut extract in a blender or food processor for 1 minute. Add the coconut mixture to the cornstarch mixture. Store mix in an airtight container.

TO USE   Stir the mix in the container, then measure out ⅔ cup and add to a saucepan. Add 2 cups whole milk and cook over low heat, stirring, until the mixture comes to a boil and thickens. Continue stirring for 1 minute, remove from the heat, and pour into individual serving dishes. The pudding will thicken further as it cools.

Makes 32 ounces of pudding

Garlic Butter

This spread is pungent, but convenient. Make sure you keep the container you store it in tightly closed or even the baking soda in your refrigerator will smell like an Italian deli.

> **1 cup (2 sticks) butter, softened**
> **6 garlic cloves, chopped**
> **2 tablespoons finely minced fresh parsley**
> **2 tablespoons chopped onions or scallions**
> **½ teaspoon freshly ground black pepper**

1. In a blender, a food processor, or by hand combine all of the ingredients and blend thoroughly.
2. Store in a tightly closed container in the refrigerator for up to 3 months, or freeze for 1 year. Or for ease of use, freeze this butter in tiny, one-serving-size portions. A plastic ice cube tray is ideal, or you might drop the mixture, by spoonfuls, onto a baking sheet, cover with plastic wrap, and freeze. After the butter is frozen solid, remove it from its container or pop the mounds off the baking sheet and store them in a plastic bag.

TO USE Freshly made or refrigerated, this butter is an ideal spread for Italian bread, see Savory Buttered Bread Sticks (page 22), or pita bread.

Use a single serving to spruce up cooked vegetables, to flavor cooked meats (especially just before or after broiling), and for tossing with freshly cooked pasta.

Makes 8 ounces garlic butter

French Herb Butter

Once you've made up a batch of this mix, store it in the freezer and use it for rice and bread spreads, as well as for vegetable, fish, and broiled or grilled meat dishes. Since the butter is intended to flavor the food to which it is added, it's a good idea to use the freshest herbs you can find.

If you don't have any fresh herbs on hand and would like to use dried herbs or spices, reduce the tablespoon to a teaspoon, taste, and adjust the seasoning as desired. You can also use Country "Butter" (page 191) to replace the butter in this recipe.

See the ideas below for individual serving suggestions. In addition, you can make your own international and foreign-flavored vegetable dishes with these butters. The variations following this recipe will get you started, but you should have your own family favorites before long.

> 1 cup (2 sticks) butter, softened
> ¼ cup chopped fresh parsley
> 1 teaspoon fresh lemon juice
> 1 tablespoon chopped fresh dill
> 1 tablespoon chopped fresh tarragon

1 teaspoon freshly ground black pepper
½ teaspoon salt

1. Cream the butter in a blender, mixer, or food processor, and add each of the ingredients separately, scraping down the sides of the jar or bowl, and blending well after each addition.

2. There are several ways to store the butter. Spread the mixture into a plastic ice cube tray, freeze for several hours, then transfer the cubes to a plastic bag. Plastic egg cartons also work quite nicely—simply pop the butter out of the used cartons once it is frozen and store in a plastic bag. (Thoroughly wash and dry the egg cartons so as to protect against possible Salmonella from the raw eggs that were originally packaged in the carton.) Or line an 8-inch-square cake pan with wax paper or plastic wrap and spread the butter into a 1-inch-thick layer. Freeze for several hours, cut into 1-inch cubes while still frozen, and store in a plastic bag. For easy use, place the butter on a sheet of plastic wrap or wax paper, roll it up into a log, and twist the ends to seal. Freeze the butter for 1 hour, then cut the log into slices. If you wish, you can slice the log and wrap each slice individually in plastic wrap and return to the freezer in a plastic bag.

TO USE   Boil or steam vegetables as usual and drain. Just before serving, toss a cube or slice of the herbed butter in with the hot vegetables.

When broiling fish, place one or more cubes of the butter on the broiling pan and put it under the broiler for 1 minute. Then place the fish on top of the butter mixture, and baste well before broiling.

If you are grilling fish, use heavy-duty aluminum foil and wrap 1 cube of the butter mixture in with the fish. Place the package on the grill and cook for 10 to 20 minutes, depending on the size of the fish.

Italian-Flavored Butter

    1 cup (2 sticks) butter, softened
    1 tablespoon olive oil
    2 garlic cloves, pressed
    1 tablespoon chopped fresh oregano
    1 tablespoon chopped fresh basil
    1 teaspoon freshly ground black pepper
    ½ teaspoon salt

Cream the butter in a blender, mixer, or food processor, and add each of the ingredients separately, scraping down the sides of the jar or bowl, and blending well after each addition. Store, or use as for French Herb Butter (page 187) on green beans, fresh boiled spinach, with freshly chopped and steamed tomatoes, onions, peppers, or zucchini.

Mexican-Flavored Butter

    1 cup (2 sticks) butter, softened
    1 tablespoon Tabasco or your favorite hot sauce
    1 tablespoon Firehouse Hot Chili Powder (page 200)
    1 tablespoon ground cumin

Cream the butter in a blender, mixer, or food processor, and add each of the ingredients separately, scraping down the sides of the jar or bowl, and blending well after each addition. Store, or use as for French Herb Butter (page 187) on chopped red tomatoes and onions, green beans, chopped lettuce, steamed cabbage, or with corn and chopped red bell peppers.

Asian-Flavored Butter

1 cup (2 sticks) butter, softened
2 tablespoons soy sauce
1 tablespoon ground ginger
1 tablespoon chopped scallions
1 teaspoon sugar

Cream the butter in a blender, mixer, or food processor, and add each of the ingredients separately, scraping down the sides of the jar or bowl, and blending well after each addition. Store, or use as for French Herb Butter (page 187) on stir-fried snow peas, water chestnuts, bamboo shoots, carrot slivers, broccoli, cauliflower, beans, or asparagus.

French-Flavored Butter

1 cup (2 sticks) butter, softened
2 tablespoons white wine
2 tablespoons chopped scallions
2 garlic cloves, pressed
1 teaspoon thyme

Cream the butter in a blender, mixer, or food processor, and add each of the ingredients separately, scraping down the sides of the jar or bowl, and blending well after each addition. Store, or use as for French Herb Butter (page 187) on freshly steamed baby peas, carrots, new potatoes, asparagus, or cauliflower.

TO USE   Top your herbed vegetables with grated cheese or 2 tablespoons of Healthy Bread Crumbs (page 46). Place under the broiler for 1 minute and serve.

Or whip any of these butters with ½ cup cottage cheese and serve with crackers as a party spread.

Herb butters are an excellent addition to scrambled eggs: mix 1 teaspoon in just before the eggs are set.

Use herb butter in place of plain butter to make a regular white sauce more interesting.

A generous chunk of herb butter can be tucked under the skin of chicken breasts or rolled-up fish fillets before broiling.

Each recipe makes about 8 ounces butter, enough for 8 servings

---

Country "Butter"

Here is a clever way to stretch margarine, while at the same time softening and enriching its flavor a bit. My mother tells me that this was one of the many ways people made do without butter during World War II. And, except for the small amount of butter in the buttermilk, you will have a spread that is relatively low in unsaturated fats, if that is a concern of yours.

> 1 pound margarine, softened
> 1 cup corn oil
> 1 cup buttermilk

Whip all of the ingredients together in a food processor or using an electric mixer. Store in a tightly covered container in the refrigerator. The spread will keep well for 1 month.

TO USE   Use this spread as the basis for any of the herb butters in this section, Sweet Butter (page 193), or some of the other savory butters and spreads listed in the index. You will save a bit more than if you used regular butter, but be careful of the consistency—reduce the corn oil, if necessary.

Makes 8 ounces country "butter"

VARIATION
◆ **Whipped Butter:** If you would like to save even more money, consider whipping your own butter or butter spreads. You can use your own Country "Butter" or any purchased butter in this recipe, but you will need a handheld electric mixer because you must keep the butter extremely cold as you whip, and the only simple way to do this is to whip the butter directly over ice.

First, let the butter warm to room temperature and place it in a bowl nestled over a bed of ice cubes. Whip the butter on high speed until it begins to harden again and lighten in color. Scrape down the sides of the bowl often, and stop when the butter begins to stick to the beaters.

You can add herbs, spices, honey, or other flavorings at this point if you wish. Scrape the butter into a crock or plastic container, cover, and refrigerate. The butter will keep for 3 weeks.

Ooh-la-la Butter

This butter is rich, decadent, and makes a wonderful spread when you feel you need pampering. You can spread this on muffins or slices of bread and then broil for a minute or two for a hot, bubbly treat.

½ cup (1 stick) butter or Country "Butter" (page
191)
½ cup honey
¼ cup sugar
¼ cup lightly packed brown sugar
1 teaspoon ground cinnamon
1 teaspoon vanilla extract or Vanilla Bean
Extract (page 205)
1 tablespoon heavy cream

Combine all of the ingredients in the jar of a food processor or in the bowl of an electric mixer and blend until
the butter is light and fluffy. Store in a tightly closed container in the refrigerator for 1 to 2 months.

Makes 8 ounces butter

VARIATION
◆ **Sweet Butter:** When the urge for something sweet strikes
you, and you want your spread to be a pretty pastel color, try
any of the following additions to the basic spread.

- ½ cup strawberries or other berries
- ½ cup chopped dates, raisins, or other dried
  fruit
- ¼ cup orange juice concentrate
- 2 tablespoons orange marmalade
- ⅓ cup whole-berry cranberry sauce

Mix and store as for Ooh-la-la Butter.

Homemade Peanut Butter

It is healthier to avoid adding salt to your recipes, especially for those foods that children eat the most, like peanut butter. However, you may find that a small amount of salt, or salted peanuts as the base of this recipe, will make the food taste more like the brands your children are used to. The fresh taste of the peanuts themselves will probably win the salt-lover over, so try the recipe first without the extra salt.

I've described several different ways to mash or pulverize the peanuts into butter, should you want to experiment. The manual methods will yield a nice crunchy spread and if you allow children to help, they will learn a bit about their favorite food.

> 2 cups dry-roasted or raw peanuts, shelled and
>   skinned
> ½ teaspoon salt
> 1 to 5 drops peanut oil (optional)

1. Process and mash the peanuts with the salt, if using, in any of the following ways:

   - Whirl the peanuts in a food processor for 90 seconds, stopping and scraping down the sides when necessary.
   - Or place the peanuts in a blender, about ¼ cup at a time, and blend for 60 seconds.
   - Or place the peanuts on a clean baking sheet and mash with a potato masher, moving the mashed peanuts to the side as you go, and adding drops of the peanut oil to the mixture as needed.

- Or mash and roll the peanuts with a rolling pin on a clean cutting board. Scrape the mixture into a bowl, and stir in additional oil if the mixture seems too dry.

2. Store the peanut butter in a clean jar or covered plastic bowl in the refrigerator. If the oil separates, stir before using. This peanut butter should keep for up to 3 months refrigerated.

Makes 16 ounces peanut butter

VARIATION

- **Cashew-Sesame Butter:** For another kind of nut butter, you might try this blend of seeds and nuts. Combine 3 tablespoons vegetable oil, 2 cups roasted cashews, and 3 tablespoons toasted sesame seeds in the jar of a blender or in a food processor and blend on medium speed. Store covered in the refrigerator for up to 2 months.

Makes 16 ounces cashew-sesame butter

- **Additional Flavors:** Try adding other ingredients to your freshly ground peanut butters and swirl them once or twice through to combine but not mix in completely. A cup of miniature marshmallows or some raisins, jam, or Basic Chocolate Sauce (page 176) would be delicious and could simplify sandwich preparation because all the ingredients for a sweet sandwich are in one jar. You could also add sliced bananas to finish off the sandwich, if desired.

Spicy Lemon Salt Substitute

There are several ways to try to cut down on your salt intake if, like me, you have a low tolerance for heavily salted foods. Spirited combinations of spices are one way, using a salt substitute as part of a recipe is another, and the easiest way to get used to the taste of less salt is to try a substitute that leaves a little salt in, as in the following two recipes.

Whether you use fresh or dried herbs, a mortar and pestle is a good way to grind the spices finely enough to sprinkle through a shaker. Or you can whirl the herbs in a blender until you have a fine mix.

¼ cup dried minced onion (see page 162)
¼ cup dried minced green pepper (see page 162)
¼ cup dried minced celery (see page 162)
5 garlic cloves, chopped
2 tablespoons grated lemon zest
2 tablespoons chopped dried parsley
2 tablespoons dried basil
1 tablespoon dried oregano
1 tablespoon dried savory
1 teaspoon dried marjoram
1 teaspoon ground coriander
1 teaspoon ground cumin

Combine all of the ingredients and process in a blender until finely chopped, about 1 minute. Stop and scrape down the sides of the blender often because the mixture will be a bit sticky at first. Store the spice mix in a tightly capped shaker jar and use in place of salt in meat and main-course recipes and on salads.

Makes 8 ounces salt substitute

Sesame Seasoning Salt

One easy way to cut down on salt is to switch your salt and pepper containers—put salt in the pepper shaker and less salt will come through the smaller holes. You will automatically cut your salt intake by half.

This variant on just plain old salt uses one of my very favorite spices, sesame seeds. I almost think it's my favorite part of sushi. Almost.

¾ cup sesame seeds
¼ cup sea salt
1 teaspoon paprika
1 teaspoon freshly ground black pepper
1 teaspoon chopped fresh chives

1. In a large skillet over medium heat, cook and stir the sesame seeds until light brown. Add the salt and cook 5 minutes more, stirring constantly. Set aside to cool.
2. Place the sesame seed mixture and the paprika, pepper, and chives in a blender and blend for 1 minute, or until the mixture is finely ground. Store in an airtight container for up to 6 months.

Makes 11 ounces seasoning salt

Sea Salt Seasoning

½ cup sea salt

2 tablespoons paprika

1 teaspoon dried parsley flakes

1 teaspoon dried basil

1 teaspoon dried oregano

1 teaspoon dried thyme

1 teaspoon freshly ground black pepper

1 teaspoon dried marjoram

1 teaspoon celery seed

1 teaspoon garlic powder

½ teaspoon curry powder (see page 67)

½ teaspoon cayenne pepper

Combine all of the ingredients in a blender and process until the herbs are finely ground and well combined. Store in a tightly covered jar on the pantry shelf. The seasoning will keep well for up to 6 months.

Great Seasonings Salad Dressing Mix

Keep this mix on your pantry shelf to combine with wine vinegar or Herbal Vinegar (page 57) and oil. The flavors will vary widely depending on the herbs in the different vinegars, but you will have a whole range of dressings with one seasoning mix.

¼ cup grated Parmesan or Pecorino Romano
   cheese

1 tablespoon paprika

2 teaspoons garlic powder

2 teaspoons celery seeds

1 teaspoon sesame seeds

½ teaspoon salt

½ teaspoon freshly ground black pepper

Mix together all of the ingredients, label, and store in a tightly closed container. This mix will keep on the pantry shelf for 1 to 2 months, or in the refrigerator for 6 months.

TO USE   Combine 2 teaspoons Great Seasonings Salad Dressing Mix, ¼ cup vinegar, and ⅔ cup vegetable oil in a jar. Cover and shake well. Transfer to a pretty cruet for serving.

Makes 5 ounces seasoning for salad dressing

VARIATIONS   Add 1 tablespoon Great Seasonings Salad Dressing Mix to ¼ cup mayonnaise for a creamy herbal dressing.

Or try adding 1 tablespoon of the mix to ¼ cup sour cream or Homemade Yogurt (page 42) for a tangy herbal dip. A few tablespoons of Tangy Mustard (page 201) will add additional spice.

Mexican Seasoning Mix

Since my family loves Mexican flavors, this seasoning mix is used constantly at our house on ground beef, mixed with cheese for topping nacho chips, and combined with sour cream for a dip.

1 cup dried minced onion (see page 162) or use
store-bought

⅓ cup beef bouillon powder

⅓ cup Firehouse Hot Chili Powder (below)

2 tablespoons ground cumin

4 teaspoons crushed red pepper flakes

1 tablespoon dried oregano

2 teaspoons garlic powder

Combine all of the ingredients and store in a cool, dry pantry for up to 4 months.

TO USE   Add 1 tablespoon to recipes calling for a Mexican flavor, or sprinkle liberally on top of foods you want to spice: 1 tablespoon mixed with chopped tomatoes and green peppers makes a tasty dip or filling for tacos.

Add 1 tablespoon to shredded cheese before melting for a dip. Serve with sour cream.

Makes 16.3 ounces seasoning

Firehouse Hot Chili Powder

If you like your chili fiery hot, you can vary this recipe to include a bit more cayenne and use hot, rather than mild, chili peppers—but label it accordingly. This powder will have a better consistency if you use a mortar and pestle to grind the peppers and coarser spices.

6 tablespoons paprika

2 tablespoons turmeric

1 tablespoon dried mild or hot chili peppers

1 teaspoon cumin

1 teaspoon oregano

½ teaspoon cayenne pepper
½ teaspoon garlic powder
½ teaspoon salt
¼ teaspoon ground cloves

Mix all of the ingredients and grind to a fine powder using a mortar and pestle, or process in your food processor or blender. The chili powder will keep for up to 6 months on the pantry shelf.

TO USE   This powder is somewhat more pungent and fresher tasting than a store-bought brand, so use a bit less.

Makes 5.5 ounces chili powder

Tangy Mustard

The ingredient that imparts the tang to the following different mustards varies from recipe to recipe. You might like the zip of horseradish over the bite of cayenne—try the versions listed here and invent your own from these ideas.

These mustards also make fantastic gifts, either alone or in combination with other spices and cheeses. Plan ahead for gift-giving by saving pretty containers and crocks for the mustards, but do not freeze these mixtures.

Spicy Horseradish Mustard

1 cup dry mustard
¾ cup white wine vinegar
⅓ cup water
¼ cup sugar

3 tablespoons lightly packed brown sugar

2 teaspoons onion salt

1 teaspoon caraway seeds

2 large eggs

1 tablespoon prepared horseradish

1. Combine all of the ingredients except for the eggs and horseradish in the top of a double boiler. Cover and let stand for 5 hours at room temperature before cooking so that the flavors will blend.

2. In a separate bowl, lightly beat the eggs and stir them into the mustard mixture. Cook the mixture slowly over low heat, stirring constantly, for 10 minutes, or until the mixture thickens.

3. Stir in the horseradish, remove from the heat, and cool for 10 minutes. Pour into a sterilized jar and refrigerate for 24 hours before using. The mustard will keep in the refrigerator for up to 3 months.

Makes 8 ounces mustard

Hot Peppery Mustard

⅔ cup beer

½ cup dry mustard

2 tablespoons water

1 tablespoon sugar

2 teaspoons white wine vinegar

1 teaspoon salt

1 teaspoon cayenne pepper

½ teaspoon turmeric

½ teaspoon ground ginger

1 large egg

1. Combine all of the ingredients, except for the egg, in the top of a double boiler. Cover and let stand for 3 hours at room temperature.
2. In a separate bowl, lightly beat the egg and stir it into the mustard mixture. Cook the mixture slowly over low heat, stirring constantly, for 10 minutes, or until the mixture thickens.
3. Remove the mustard from the heat and cool for 10 minutes. Pour into a sterilized jar and refrigerate for 24 hours before using. The mustard will keep in the refrigerator for up to 3 months.

Makes 16 ounces mustard

VARIATIONS   Try adding 2 tablespoons of Great Seasonings Salad Dressing Mix (page 198) to one of the mixtures before stirring in the egg. Replace the sugar with the same amount of honey to achieve a different flavor.

Sweet Berry Syrups

You can use these syrups on Quick Mabel, the Pancakes! (page 252) or Crepes Diem (page 137). In addition, they taste wonderful over vanilla ice cream or swirled through Vanilla Pudding Mix (see page 183).

Blueberry Syrup

> 3 cups blueberries
> 3 cups sugar
> 1 cup water
> ¼ cup fresh lemon juice

1. Wash and drain the blueberries. Crush the berries in a bowl, or process for 1 minute in a food processor or blender.
2. Place the puree in an enamel or nonreactive pan and stir in the sugar and the water. Cook over medium heat for 30 minutes, stirring regularly.
3. Remove from the heat and stir in the lemon juice.
4. Strain the mixture through a coffee filter or a cheesecloth-lined strainer and pour the syrup into a sterilized jar. Discard the pulp. Cool the syrup before using and store in the refrigerator for up to 6 months.

Makes 32 ounces syrup

VARIATIONS   Almost any kind of berry can be substituted for the blueberries. You should add half the sugar called for, taste, and add more sugar if you think the berries will need more sweetening.

Sweetened Condensed Milk

I've always believed that this convenient pantry item only comes in cans, boiled into them with some sort of magical factory formula. Imagine the fun of making it up fresh when this, and only this, form of milk will do in a recipe.

2 cups instant nonfat dry milk
1½ cups sugar
⅔ cup boiling water
6 tablespoons (¾ stick) unsalted butter, melted
    and slightly cooled

1. Mix the dry milk and sugar together and then slowly add the boiling water. Stir in the melted butter.
2. Whip in a blender, or by hand, until smooth.
3. Store the milk in the refrigerator for 1 week, or freeze for up to 6 months.

Makes 20 ounces sweetened condensed milk

Vanilla Bean Extract

This interesting brew is very much like the liquid we call vanilla extract, and yet it is special. It isn't as potent, but it is smooth, with a good vanilla flavor. Use it in recipes that call for just a touch of vanilla.

> **3 or 4 vanilla beans**
> **½ cup brandy**

1. Cut the vanilla beans into small pieces, being careful not to lose any of the pod or the little black seeds.
2. Drop the pieces into a clean jar and cover with the brandy. Cover with a tight-fitting lid and keep in a dark place, shaking every third day or so. The extract will be ready in about 2 weeks. A touch more brandy can be added if the beans seem too potent. The mixture can be added to indefinitely.

TO USE   Use just as you would regular vanilla extract, but taste to make sure the brandy flavor is not too strong.

Makes 4 ounces extract

Polka-Dotties:
The Glynnis McCann Special

Here's a question, best asked before the age of the Internet. Who was Polka Dottie? Answer, she was a character on a children's TV show that is still buried in the mists of my memory called *Rootie Kazootie*.

Polka Dottie and Rootie sang a song together, which you can still find somewhere on the Internet. In honor of that puppet character on one of the great television shows of the 1950s, here is a recipe for something delightful named after her.

I love this recipe because you can eat it up as a snack, hang it on your Christmas tree as a decoration, hand it out to friends as a party favor, or wear it around your neck and dance to the Polka Dottie Rootie Kazootie song. If you have a candy thermometer, a handy little utensil, you should definitely not use it in the microwave. Test the temperature immediately after removing the bowl.

> 16 cups popped corn
> 1 cup sugar
> ½ cup light corn syrup
> ⅓ cup water
> ⅓ teaspoon salt
> 1 teaspoon vanilla extract
> ¼ cup (½ stick) butter or margarine
> 1 cup candied cherries, gum drops (Gummy
>   Bears will do), or brightly colored jelly beans

1. Combine the sugar, corn syrup, water, and salt in a ceramic bowl and microwave on medium for 90 seconds. Stir, and re-

Polka-Dotties

peat until sugar is completely dissolved. You can't overheat to get sugar to dissolve, so take it slowly. Ever try making rock candy? Same thing. This has to be a gradual thing.

2. Continue to microwave until the temperature of the mixture reaches 254°F on a candy thermometer, which means the mixture is ready. You can also test this out with just a pinch of it; the mixture forms into a hard ball when dropped into a cup of cold water.

3. Remove from the oven and add the vanilla extract.

4. Divide the popcorn between 2 baking pans, spread the popcorn out, and pat the mixture evenly onto the 2 pans of popcorn, stirring each to coat the popcorn evenly.

5. Grease your hands with a little cooking oil or butter and form the coated popcorn into 4-inch balls while the mixture is still warm and malleable.

6. Press candied cherries, gum drops, jelly beans, or other bright candy onto the surface of each popcorn ball.

7. Let the popcorn balls cool. Wrap each ball in clear plastic wrap, tie the end closed with a bright ribbon, and:

  • Hang from your Christmas tree.
  • Hang from the holly branches in your house or around your front door.
  • Hand out to friends and children.
  • Just eat them right up and forget about the decorations.

You can see how sometimes you can have fun with food by realizing that something colorful and tasty can have multiple functions.

Makes about 6 to 12 popcorn balls, depending on size

9

• PSYCHOLOGY • MIND •
• SUPERNATURAL • PARANORMAL •

Uri's Bent Spoon Bread

Fruit-Nut Balls

Silly Cereal

Popcorn-Nut Munchy Mixture

Jiffy Sweet Rolls

Maple Biscuits

Late-Night Tasty Squares

Brownies! Brownies Fix Everything!

Brandied Peaches

Spiced and Fancy After-Dinner Coffee

We all know that a spoonful of sugar helps the bitter truths go down, and here in this chapter we have gathered the sweet, the silly, and the fun treats. Feel free to indulge in one of these little helpers if you get too stressed to cope with the ever-increasing pace of today's news.

Professionally, I'm a late-night guy. My whole day is geared to late night, even when I'm not on the air. I can empathize with my listeners, because I share their dark-city environment, their world at night, the long-haul truck drivers, the police officers on the graveyard shift, the doctors and nurses working late shifts in the E-rooms through the night, and just about anybody whose job it is to work through the night.

It's a funny thing that happens to professional late-night people. Your entire circadian rhythm changes so that break-fast, lunch, and dinner seem different than for folks who get up right at dawn, fix breakfast for the kids, clean up, dress up, jump in a car or on a bus or a train, and head off to work, coming home during standard time, as it's getting dark or after dark. You live in a city of perpetual night.

All of this, for the purposes of cooking up treats, means that what I might call a late-night treat can also be an early daybreak treat, a tide-me-over-before-dinner treat, or even a prebreakfast breakfast treat. And these are some of the recipes for my favorite treats that I am writing about in this chapter. I call them "jiffy treats" because even if part of the preparation takes longer than a jiffy, when you pop it in the microwave or toaster oven, it's ready in a jiffy.

Some of these may have enough sugar to make your blood glucose meters explode, and your test strips wither from the intensity. For those of you who want to avoid this, you can replace sugar with either Stevia or Splenda or another sugar substitute. Or, where possible, you can go cold turkey.

If a sweet diversion doesn't do the trick, how about brandy? As screenwriter Ogden Nash so famously said: "Candy is dandy, but liquor is quicker."

Uri's Bent Spoon Bread

We all know that psychic personality Uri Geller is best known for his ability to bend spoons. Here is a fun way to celebrate his abilities.

> One 15-ounce can corn, drained
> One 15-ounce can creamed corn
> 1 cup sour cream
> 2 large eggs, lightly beaten
> ½ cup (1 stick) butter, melted
> One 8.5-ounce box corn muffin/cornbread mix
> ½ teaspoon salt
> ¼ teaspoon freshly ground black pepper
> Ground cinnamon

1. Preheat the oven to 350°F. Grease a 8 by 8-inch ovenproof baking dish.
2. In a large bowl, combine the corn, creamed corn, sour cream, eggs, butter, corn muffin mix, salt, and pepper.
3. Place the corn mixture in the prepared baking dish. Bake for 45 minutes.
4. Serve warm with a sprinkling of ground cinnamon.

Makes one 8 by 8-inch cornbread cake

Fruit-Nut Balls

Let your kids have a hand, literally, with this recipe. It's fun to mix everything up, and the children can get a whole new appreciation of "candy" if they make up some of their own. You and the kids can make it up in advance and then when they're off to bed, you can eat it up when listening to *Coast* late at night.

⅔ cup Sweetened Condensed Milk (page 204)
2 teaspoons Vanilla Bean Extract (page 205)
¼ cup finely chopped nuts
⅓ cup shredded unsweetened coconut
⅓ cup raisins
½ cup dried fruit of your choice
½ cup quick-cooking rolled oats

1. Mix all of the ingredients together and let the mixture sit for 30 minutes. Form into balls.
2. Preheat the oven to 325°F. Grease a baking sheet well.
3. Butter your hands and shape the mixture into small balls. Place the balls on the prepared baking sheet and bake for 12 to 15 minutes.
4. Remove from the baking sheet before the candy has completely cooled and transfer the balls to a wire rack to cool completely. Store in a tightly closed container. The candy will keep for 2 to 4 weeks.

Makes 18 ounces fruit-nut balls

Silly Cereal

Remember that great scene in *Seinfeld* when Jerry says to his date that he loves to have cereal at night? Who says you can't have cereal at night? Who says you can't make your own, store it, and have it whenever you feel the need? Or you can make up a batch of this cereal for one of those days when you have a roomful of children and a morning full of cartoons. This cereal is best eaten right away. Serve with cold milk and sliced fresh fruit. Extra cereal may be stored in an airtight container for another time or just eaten as a snack.

> ½ cup Rainbow Drink Mix (page 132) (a mixture
>   of milk and any powdered milk flavoring
>   such as strawberry milk)
> 2 tablespoons honey, warmed
> 2 cups plain wheat, corn, or rice cereal
> ½ cup chopped dried fruit
> ½ cup miniature marshmallows

Combine the Rainbow Drink Mix with the warmed honey. Pour over the cereal and toss until the cereal is completely covered. Stir in the dried fruit and marshmallows and serve.

Makes 16 ounces cereal

Popcorn-Nut Munchy Mixture

OK, so we've gone from pure health with Fat-Free Faux Corn (page 50) to pure stealth with this munch treat. For those of you not on a diet and young enough not to worry about pesky things like cholesterol levels or calories, here's the fully leaded version of a popcorn treat.

This popcorn is a wonderful accompaniment to an old movie on television. If you want the mixture to be on the sweet side, use plain, dry-roasted peanuts and unsalted butter. If you want to add a bit of a salty tang to the mixture, use salted butter and salted peanuts.

12 cups popped corn
1½ cups peanuts
½ cup honey
½ cup (1 stick) butter

1. Preheat the oven to 300°F.
2. Mix together the popcorn and nuts in a very big bowl. Warm the honey and butter together over low heat until the butter is melted. Pour the honey-butter mixture over the popcorn-nut mixture. Toss to mix well.
3. Spread the mixture in a large baking pan and bake for 20 minutes, stirring once or twice during the baking. Cool and break into chunks before serving or storing in an air-tight container. The mixture will keep for 2 weeks on the pantry shelf.

VARIATIONS A mixture of cashews, walnuts, and other nuts of your choice added to the above recipe will also taste delicious.

A low-calorie version of this munchy mixture can be made by popping your corn, without oil, in a microwave oven. Pour ½ cup unpopped kernels into a paper bag, sprinkle in a tablespoon of salt substitute, and add a dash of water.

Jiffy Sweet Rolls

If you like my Late-Night Tasty Squares (page 218) and are intrigued by the concept of Schmageggies (page 153), you will love my sweet rolls made in a jiffy. This is a treat for any time of day that will take you about five minutes to make, but will give you a good feeling that will last throughout the day or night.

Do you have a microwave in your kitchen at work? Make

these up in advance the night before, bring your walnut or peanut meats, butter, and honey and brown sugar in separate little containers and make these rolls up at work. You may get promoted very quickly.

This is also a great recipe for kids if they like honey and brown sugar and know how to open a package of brown-and-serve rolls.

1 package brown-and-serve rolls
½ cup (1 stick) butter or margarine
2 tablespoons honey
¼ cup packed brown sugar
1 cup chopped walnuts or peanuts

1. Place the rolls on a flat microwave-safe dish and top each roll with a pat of butter and a spoonful of honey and brown sugar. Microwave on medium-high for 2 minutes, or until the butter melts.
2. Remove from the microwave and top the rolls with the nuts. Return the pan to the microwave and cook for 1 minute more. Serve piping hot.

Makes anywhere from 4 to 6 with a single package. My advice is to have a few packages at the ready because these go fast.

Maple Biscuits

If you are swearing off sugar, you can get sugar-free pancake syrup at the supermarket and use it in this recipe instead. Or you can be a purist and use only pure maple syrup from Maine or Vermont. Whatever you do, you'll like this recipe from the old

Klondike Gold Rush days updated for today's microwaves and family lifestyles.

These biscuits are great to tinker around with, they taste great anytime, and are phenomenally easy to make. Truth is, one of the fun parts of doing my show from St. Louis is that I can run upstairs and put together these treats without waiting to drive home, which is what I do when I broadcast from our studio in Los Angeles.

> 1 cup Biscuit Baking Mix (page 29)
> ½ cup whole milk or water
> 1 tablespoon butter
> Maple syrup, sugar-free pancake syrup, or
>   another flavored topping such as vanilla or
>   raspberry syrup

1. Combine the biscuit mix and milk or water in a bowl and stir with a fork until the dough follows the fork around the bowl.
2. Knead the dough just a few times with your hands to get the feel of handling it.
3. Drop small handfuls of the dough onto a microwave-safe sheet, making sure to leave enough room for the handfuls of dough to rise and spread.
4. Microwave on medium for 4 to 5 minutes or, if you cannot set the power level of your microwave, just until the dough begins to feel firm to the touch. If you're doing this with your kids, they will probably overcook it the first few times, but they'll get the hang of it so keep encouraging them. Maybe even give them a few batches to practice with, which is what I've done with my grandchildren. Practice also teaches kids or anyone else you're demonstrating this recipe to how to make consistently sized dough shapes. Too big and too close on the baking sheet, and you get a loaf. Too tiny, and you wind up with overcooked poppers.

5. Remove from the microwave and, while still hot, top each roll with a pat or dollop of butter and pour on the syrup. Return the biscuits to the microwave and cook on low for 1 minute, or until the butter melts. Serve hot.

Makes 6 to 8 biscuits

VARIATIONS   For variation's sake, instead of maple, vanilla, or raspberry syrup, try using store-bought cake frosting in any flavor to top your biscuits. Or mix and match.

You can even top the syrup or frosting with store-bought sugar sprinkles just like you'd top a cake. That, too, is a fun activity for kids.

You can even train your older kids to make these biscuits themselves, or you can make them together, so that everyone can enjoy the experience.

Late-Night Tasty Squares

These little goodies are sweetness bombs. I call them late-night, your kids and you may call them morning or breakfast squares. Either way, they're quick and tasty and you'll love them. Not only will you love them, but you'll want to teach your kids how to make them in the microwave, and leave some of the ingredients out for them, like honey, butter, cocoa, and brown sugar. That way they can make their own tasty breakfast squares while you lounge in bed on a Sunday morning thinking of the thousand reasons there is no impetus for you to get up.

4 slices white or whole wheat bread
4 tablespoons butter or margarine

1 tablespoon honey, preferably from the farmers'
    market because the farmer knows the bees
1 teaspoon ground cinnamon
1 tablespoon granulated brown sugar (optional)
2 tablespoons cocoa powder (sweetened or
    unsweetened, your choice) (optional)

1. Arrange the individual slices of bread on a microwave-safe tray and top each slice with a pat of butter. Microwave on low heat for 2 minutes or until the butter starts to melt.
2. Spread each slice with honey, and sprinkle with cinnamon and brown sugar or cocoa or both.
3. Microwave on low for 1½ minutes and let cool just a bit before removing from the microwave. Kids should wait a full minute so they don't get burned by the tray.

Makes 4 servings, but you can eat all of them yourself

This is a great 5-minute treat even if you have to start from scratch. Prepackage your butter and it will go even faster. Wrap the butter in foil, and leave conspicuously on the refrigerator shelf so little fingers don't squoosh the butter in their early morning eating frenzy.

Brownies! Brownies Fix Everything!

Keeping this mix on hand can really help if a chocolate attack comes—trust me—in the middle of the night and you want to go about making brownies quietly, alone, undisturbed. Once you've got the mix waiting there in the pantry, the rest of the job is very quiet.

Brownies

---

① ② 3 MONTHS

FUDGIE CHEWY BROWNIES

PEANUT BUTTER BROWNIES

---

① ②

4 cups sugar
2½ cups all-purpose flour
1½ cups unsweetened cocoa powder
2 teaspoons baking powder
1½ teaspoons salt
2 cups shortening

1. In a large bowl, mix together all of the dry ingredients. Add the shortening by spoonfuls, cutting it in with a pastry blender or two knives, or do this in a food processor.
2. Store the mix in a tightly covered container in the pantry. If you have many children around, it might help to label this one "Health Food," to preserve the mix a bit longer. If there are no children around, the mix will keep for up to 3 months in dry weather.

Fudgie Chewy Brownies

3 cups Basic Brownie Mix (see above)
2 large eggs
1 teaspoon Vanilla Bean Extract (page 205)
¼ cup Basic Chocolate Sauce (page 176)
½ cup chocolate chips

Peanut Butter Brownies

3 cups Basic Brownie Mix
2 large eggs
1 teaspoon Vanilla Bean Extract (page 205)
½ cup peanut butter chips

1. Preheat the oven to 350°F. Butter an 8-inch square pan.
2. Combine all of the ingredients in a bowl and stir to mix thoroughly. Pour into the prepared pan and bake for 30

minutes, or until a knife inserted in the center comes out clean.

Makes approximately 12 brownies

VARIATIONS   You can also add one or more of the following ingredients to any of the brownie recipes:

- ½ cup chopped walnuts
- ½ cup pulverized butter brickle
- ½ cup shredded coconut
- ½ cup chopped dates or raisins
- ½ cup crumbled chocolate candy bar

Brandied Peaches

This recipe can get you a lot of mileage. These are delicious served with ham. You can develop a light dessert salad around them with just some lettuce and parsley, you can build a dessert around them with vanilla ice cream, and you can also give them away as a nice holiday gift.

If you decide to make a gift of brandied peaches, they should be made well in advance of holiday or gift-giving time. Since peaches are plentiful in late summer, particularly on the East Coast, you will want to take advantage of their low prices then and make up your jars, but because the flavors must mellow and stew awhile, you will have to wait until Christmas or the New Year to enjoy this treat.

> **2 pounds peaches**
> **2 cups sugar**

2 cups water
Brandy

1. Peel, halve, and pit the peaches.
2. Place the sugar and water in a saucepan, bring to a boil, and boil for 10 minutes. Add the peaches, and simmer for 10 minutes.
3. Pour off the syrup into a measuring cup and combine with an equal quantity of brandy.
4. Pack the peaches in sterilized, wide-mouth glass jars without crowding them too tightly. Pour the syrup-brandy mixture over the peaches to cover. Close the jars tightly and put them away on a cool, dark pantry shelf for 6 months.

TO USE   One of the best ways to enjoy your brandied peaches is to pour them over vanilla ice cream and add a dollop of sweetened whipped cream if you like.

Save every bit of the liquid from your peaches and you can add more fruit throughout the year.

Makes 32 ounces brandied peaches

Spiced and Fancy After-Dinner Coffee

When the show is extra-special, why not make the coffee that ends the hour special, too? Or, if you're dieting and want to forgo fattening desserts, try one of the following fancy coffees to quell your sweet tooth.

4 cups freshly brewed black coffee
4 whole cloves
1 cinnamon stick

As soon as the coffee is brewed and still piping hot, place the spices in a decanter or Thermos, pour in the coffee, and let it infuse for about 10 minutes.

TO USE   Pour the spiced coffee, without removing the spices, and serve with a dollop of whipped cream dusted with ground cinnamon, or try adding a spoonful of orange cordial or coffee liqueur.

Makes 4 servings coffee

VARIATIONS   To freshly brewed coffee, add 1 tablespoon finely grated orange zest or Vanilla Bean Extract (page 205).

Try adding 1 teaspoon Basic Chocolate Sauce (page 176) and topping with crushed mint.

10

• SCIENCE • SPACE • TECHNOLOGY •

Surefire Waffles
Presto English Muffin or French Bread Pizza
Quick Pizza
A Biscuit Bonanza
Turkey Sausage Sandwiches on Torpedo Rolls
Reese's Fajitas
The Ultimate Turkey and Capicola Sub
Turkey Chili Sandwich on a Bun
Fun Dates: The Webmaster's Delight

The selections in this chapter are my idea of what the nerds, the hackers, the science dweebs, and the harassed programmers like to snack on. In other words, my listeners!

It might be lore, but it has been said that the best way to get programmers to settle down to work is to lock them away and keep the key. Then, to make sure they keep on working, their minders used to push flat food such as pita and cheese slices under the door.

We're not that cruel, so for all those rationally minded listeners, we provide hearty, well-rounded alternatives to the flat-earth option: two kinds of quick pizza, sumptuous messy sandwiches, and for our forever-alone listeners, fun dates from our always hard-working webmasters.

Surefire Waffles

If science teaches us anything, it's that there's nothing we can truly be sure about. Think the Sphinx is old? Then they discover Göbekli Tepe and add a few more thousand years to the puzzle.

So, waffle much, Mr. Scientist? Let's eat our words.

This recipe makes really big waffles that hold together. If you make a double batch of waffles, you can wrap the extra ones and store them in the freezer. Then, for a quick breakfast, pop the frozen waffles into the toaster, toaster oven, or microwave without defrosting.

> 2 cups Biscuit Baking Mix (page 29)
> 2 tablespoons vegetable oil
> 1 large egg
> 1⅓ cups whole milk

1. Combine all of the ingredients in a bowl and beat until smooth.
2. Preheat your waffle iron and pour in the batter according to the manufacturer's instructions for your waffle iron and close the lid. Bake until the steaming stops.

Makes 6 waffles

VARIATION   For dessert or Belgian waffles, add 2 tablespoons sugar to the recipe and serve the waffles with an ice cream topping.

Presto English Muffin or French Bread Pizza

When all of the pizza delivery places are closed, and you're scrounging around the kitchen for something, anything, to satisfy that pizza craving, remember you can always cobble together a quick pizza snack on an English muffin. If you want to get fancy, use a long slice of French bread or a torpedo roll. You can microwave your pizza or heat it up in your toaster oven or even your regular oven.

> **English muffin, or torpedo or sub roll, or French bread**
> **Olive oil**
> **Jar of your favorite tomato sauce**
> **Provolone or mozzarella cheese sliced or shredded**
> **Favorite toppings such as pepperoni, mushrooms, garlic**
> **Dried oregano and/or parsley, for sprinkling**

1. Preheat the oven or toaster oven to 350°F.
2. Split your English muffin, then toast lightly.
3. Brush the muffin with olive oil.
4. Spoon on as much of your sauce as you like. You can also use store-bought pizza sauce. My favorite is puttanesca sauce because I like the olives and capers.
5. Spread on the provolone or mozzarella cheese.
6. Add your toppings, and sprinkle on some oregano and parsley.

Presto English Muffin or French Bread Pizza

VARIATIONS:

7. Bake for 5 minutes, or until you see the cheese thoroughly melted. Serve nice and hot.

Makes 1 English muffin pizza

VARIATIONS
- **French Bread or Torpedo Roll Pizza:** If making French bread or torpedo roll pizza, you can get extra flavor by first slicing up some fresh garlic or using store-bought garlic in oil and heating it in a frying pan with a thin layer of olive oil. When the garlic just starts to brown, put the French bread or torpedo roll, face down, in the oil and press down with a spatula. Let the bread sizzle for a couple of minutes but don't let it burn.

Follow the steps above, adding your cheeses, toppings, oregano, and parsley. Bake for 5 minutes in your preheated oven. Sit back, listen to our guest or the callers, and enjoy your 10-minute snack.

To cook in a microwave, prepare as above, but when you are ready to melt the cheeses and heat the toppings, microwave on high for 3 minutes, or until the cheeses are completely melted. Rotate, and microwave for 1 minute more. Let cool in the microwave for 30 seconds, then remove.
- **Turkey Hawaiian Pizza:** You can vary this recipe in hundreds of ways. As we suggest in our turkey chapter, that's with turkey, not for turkeys, you can add turkey and pineapple to your pizza with or without cheese, or with cheese and no tomato sauce for a white Hawaiian or straight Hawaiian pizza.
- **Real or Veggie Sausage or Meatball Pizza:** You can add real sausage or veggie sausage, real meatballs or veggie meatballs, or just about any topping you want, including garlic, mushrooms, and even anchovies straight from the tin. And you can do it without adding too many minutes to the preparation time.

Quick Pizza

Here is a handy, thick-crusted pizza that is so easy to create that even the child who has a hankering for pizza can make it for himself. Add a little sauce and cheese and you have a fine after-school snack.

> **2 cups Biscuit Baking Mix (page 29)**
> **½ cup cold water**
> **1 cup Basic Tomato Sauce (page 27)**
> **½ cup shredded mozzarella cheese**
> **½ teaspoon dried oregano**
> **½ teaspoon garlic powder**
> **Salt and freshly ground black pepper**

1. Preheat the oven to 425°F.
2. In a bowl, stir together the baking mix and water until a soft dough forms. Roll out or pat the dough into a 12-inch circle or square on an ungreased baking sheet. Pinch up the edge of the circle to form a ½-inch rim.
3. Spread the tomato sauce over the dough, then sprinkle with the cheese and seasonings.
4. Bake for 20 to 25 minutes until the crust is golden brown.

Makes 1 small pizza, about 12 inches

VARIATION Never let not having a certain ingredient stop you from making a pizza. Around our neighborhood, some delicious pizza pies have been made from what some would consider to be strange items. For example, try brushing the crust with olive oil and top it with braised broccoli and mushrooms and lots of cheese.

A Biscuit Bonanza

My favorite thing about a biscuit is the fact that I can eat it with one hand and just keep puttering with my computer or sound equipment with the other. It's a dream to be able to eat and work at the same time.

The simple biscuits that follow are easy to make, and if you don't have any milk on hand, you can use water or reconstituted instant nonfat dried milk. For variety, add fillings of your choice, sweet toppings, or try my Latvian grandmother's special biscuits, which are absolutely heavenly.

Quick Rolled Biscuits

2 cups Biscuit Baking Mix (page 29)
⅔ cup whole milk

1. Preheat the oven to 400°F.
2. In a bowl, stir together the mix and milk and beat until a soft dough forms. If the dough feels too sticky, add a bit more mix, up to ¼ cup.
3. Turn the dough out onto a surface lightly dusted with a bit more of the baking mix or just plain flour. Roll the dough into a ball and knead gently 10 times. Roll the dough out to a thickness of ½ inch and cut into 2-inch circles or squares.
4. Place on an ungreased baking sheet and brush the tops with milk to help them brown. Bake for 8 to 10 minutes.

Dropped Biscuits

    2 cups Biscuit Baking Mix (page 29)
    1 cup whole milk

Follow steps 1 and 2 in Quick Rolled Biscuits. The mixture will be a bit looser than the dough for regular biscuits. Drop by spoonfuls onto an ungreased baking sheet and bake for 8 to 10 minutes.

Sweet Biscuits

    2 cups Biscuit Baking Mix (page 29)
    ⅔ cup whole milk
    2 tablespoons Country "Butter" (page 191)
    ¼ cup Cinnamon-Sugar (page 181)

Follow the instructions for either Quick Rolled or Dropped Biscuits. Just before baking, brush the biscuit tops with melted butter and then dust with Cinnamon-Sugar.

Sprinkled Biscuits

    2 cups Biscuit Baking Mix (page 29)
    ⅔ cup whole milk, plus 2 tablespoons milk
    ¼ cup poppy, sesame, or caraway seeds

Follow the instructions for either Quick Rolled or Dropped Biscuits. Just before baking, brush the biscuit tops with milk and then dust with seeds.

Filled Biscuits

    2 cups Biscuit Baking Mix (page 29)

⅔ cup whole milk

2 tablespoons Country "Butter" (page 191),
   melted

½ cup chopped vegetables, tuna, or another
   meat or vegetable filling of your choice

Follow the mixing and baking instructions for Quick Rolled Biscuits. Just before baking, brush one biscuit circle for the bottom with melted butter, add a teaspoon of chopped vegetables, chicken, tuna, or another filling, top with another biscuit circle, pinch the sides, and brush with milk to seal.

Latvian Biscuits

1 small onion

2 slices bacon

2 tablespoons Country "Butter" (page 191),
   melted

2 cups Biscuit Baking Mix (page 29)

⅔ cup whole milk

1. Chop the onion and bacon into small pieces. In a skillet, melt the butter over low heat. Add the onion and bacon and cook them together until the onion is translucent and the bacon is cooked but not crispy.

2. Meanwhile, prepare the dough for Quick Rolled Biscuits. Spoon the onion and bacon from the pan and add, without draining, to the dough just before kneading. Proceed as for Quick Rolled Biscuits, brushing the tops with a bit of the bacon grease before baking.

Each recipe makes 10 medium biscuits

Turkey Sausage Sandwiches on Torpedo Rolls

Remember the character of Clemenza in *The Godfather*, Don Corleone's main henchman in the "family" business? Remember after the Corleone family had gone to the wall during the war with the other New York families how Clemenza explained to a young Michael Corleone (Al Pacino) how to fry up sausage for a quick meal? You can prepare the same recipe with turkey sausage—my favorite—and here is how to do it.

Of course, in *The Godfather*, Clemenza added some crackling dry white wine to the frying sausage, Soave, Pinot Grigio, Frascati, or Verdicchio. But unless the Tattaglias are breeching the outside wall of the compound, you can make this dish alcohol-free.

> One 16-ounce package turkey sausage, hot or
>   sweet, or a mix
> 1 teaspoon extra-virgin olive oil
> 1 garlic clove
> 1 green or red bell pepper, seeded and thinly
>   sliced
> 1 medium onion, thinly sliced
> 1 package hoagie rolls, preferably imported
>   from Philly
> 1 Italian plum tomato, sliced
> Pinch of salt and freshly ground black pepper
> Mustard, or more olive oil and some balsamic
>   vinegar, or 1 jar marinara or puttanesca sauce
>   (optional)

1. In a saucepan, bring some water to a rolling boil until it bubbles vigorously. Split the sausage lengthwise down the middle and pierce the pork casing with a fork.

2. Add the sausage to the water and adjust the heat to maintain a medium boil, skimming the scum off the top, and cook until the sausage floats to the surface. While the sausage is cooking, heat the oil in a skillet over high heat and add the garlic. Cook the garlic just until it starts to brown.

3. Add the pepper and onion slices to the skillet and stir like a madman.

4. When the sausage is cooked, slice each piece in two lengthwise and add it to the peppers and onions in the skillet. Fry the entire mixture until the sausage is nicely browned.

5. Remove from the heat and build your sandwich by placing sausage on your torpedo (think, hoagie) roll and add the peppers and onions between the sausage halves. Top off with tomatoes. Sprinkle with salt and pepper.

6. Now you have lots of choices: mustard, if that's your proclivity, more olive oil and some balsamic vinegar, or even tomato sauce, either marinara or puttanesca. The only problem with this recipe is that you probably won't be able to stop eating. It's that good.

Makes 6 sandwiches

Reese's Fajitas

Fajitas can be some of the easiest things to cook up either for yourself and friends or for a crowd. Let's say that you're having friends over for a night of listening to one of my special guests on *Coast*. Maybe it's one of my end-of-days experts, a survivalist expert, Stan Friedman on the veracity of the MJ-12 documents, or Loren Coleman on searching for Big Foot.

These guys always prompt a heavy discussion, and nothing feeds a controversial debate among friends gathering for a *Coast* listening session any better than the makings of a fajita on the table and a stack of corn or wheat tortilla wraps along with as much hot sauce as you can handle.

You can prepare a smorgasbord of fajita fixings, spreading them out buffet style for folks to pick, or you can prepare individual fajita wraps for each guest. Or you can simply prepare one for yourself and settle back into the conversation on the radio. You can see that this is a great meal for outdoor cooking, or just plain outdoor eating, and works for picnics with your hibachi grill or at the park. You don't need a special occasion for fajitas.

I call this "Reese's Fajitas" after my friend's little granddaughter because this is her absolutely favorite meal.

    1 to 2 tablespoons olive oil, depending on the
        number of servings and how long you are
        going to keep the ingredients on the heat
    2 garlic cloves, very thinly sliced
    2 bell peppers, one red and one green, very, very
        thinly sliced
    2 Spanish onions, very thinly sliced
    1 tablespoon chili powder
    1 tablespoon ground cumin or whole cumin
        seed
    ¼ teaspoon cayenne pepper, or Tabasco or your
        favorite hot sauce
    1 or more pounds thinly sliced turkey or
        chicken breast, depending on the number of
        servings
    ½ teaspoon salt (These fixings can get very salty
        on their own, so I like to be very circumspect
        with the amount of salt I use.)

½ teaspoon freshly ground black pepper (It's easier to use ground pepper straight from the jar, but I like to use whole peppercorns and grind them myself, just like the servers do in high-end restaurants. It's fresher tasting.)

4 to 8 ounces shredded combination of Colby-Jack and cheddar cheese, depending on your taste for cheese (The combination of cheeses makes this dish because the taste just explodes when these cheeses melt together on the hot turkey or chicken slices.)

1 or more packages of soft tortillas, wheat or corn, your choice

1 or more packages of store-bought crunchy taco shells, mainly for variety (You can make a fajita tortilla wrap or you can make a fajita taco. For my taste, which is strictly personal, I like my melted cheese over peppers and onions topped with tomatoes on a crunchy taco shell. However, I like my sliced turkey wrapped up in a soft and hot corn tortilla.)

2 to 3 fresh tomatoes, depending on the number of servings, thinly sliced

Crushed red pepper flakes

10 large lettuce leaves, red for color, green for shopping convenience, your choice

2 tablespoons chopped fresh cilantro, or straight from the spice jar

One 16-ounce container sour cream

1 jar or more of your absolutely favorite salsa, mild, medium, or hot, smooth or chunky, your choice (For me, I like the peach salsa or raspberry salsa, but then I'm the kind of guy who loves to mix sweet with salty.)

1. Heat the olive oil and one clove of the sliced garlic in a large skillet over high heat. If you are preparing your fajitas at the table instead of on the stovetop, you can use a large electric skillet on its highest setting. Or you can use a regular large skillet over an electric hotplate or table-top burner.

2. While the olive oil and garlic are heating, wash and thoroughly dry the peppers. If still wet, the peppers will splatter hot droplets of water when they hit the oil, all of which can burn.

3. When the olive oil starts bubbling up, reduce the heat and add the peppers and onions, browning them slightly. Immediately add the chili powder, cumin, and cayenne.

4. Transfer the peppers and onions to a serving dish. Add the turkey or chicken slices to the hot oil and cook, stirring, until heated through. Season with salt and pepper to taste.

5. Grate the cheese or cut into thin, narrow slices to spread over the fajitas after you've piled on the fixin's so that the cheese melts over the fajita.

6. Warm up the tortillas and taco shells in your oven, toaster oven, or microwave. I prefer a toaster oven because you can easily overcook tortillas in the microwave, turning them into sheet rock. If you decide to use a microwave, I suggest you wrap the tortillas in a moistened paper towel and microwave for 15 seconds. That way they will turn out warm and soft.

7. Place the peppers and onions and tomatoes in separate dishes. Place the turkey or chicken slices in a separate dish. Set your tortillas alongside a small dish of red pepper flakes or cayenne and set out your garnishes and toppings. Open the floodgates and let your guests have at it, building their own fajitas.

VARIATIONS We're talking about turkey and chicken here, but you can also prepare beef fajitas by cooking your own favorite cut of beef, such as brisket, slicing it very thinly, and following the steps above. If spending hours cooking your brisket seems onerous, especially late at night, try this.

Use any one of the store-bought, precooked brisket, tri-tip, or roast beef packages, either from Tyson or Hormel, follow the microwave or oven directions, then prepare just as you would the turkey or chicken.

For your own Cinco de Mayo picnic, no matter what your ethnic background, cook up all three—turkey, chicken, and beef—and set them out in separate dishes.

The Ultimate Turkey and Capicola Sub

Here's a variation on the classic South Philly and South Jersey hoagie. It's a sandwich on a torpedo (hoagie) roll loaded with meat and cheese, but with added slices of turkey, which you can replace or even complete with slices of chicken.

If you're using packaged turkey slices from the supermarket, you can also vary the flavor with either smoked, mesquite, honey, or even peppered turkey. I'm recommending the amount of meat slices on this dish, but if you were an avid reader of the "Blondie" comic strip and remember what the famous "Dagwood" sandwich was, you can load this bad boy right up with sliced meat and enjoy the ride while listening to *Coast*.

By the way, even if you are inspired to call in with a comment, don't call in with your mouth full. First chew, then swallow, then call. It makes for a more comprehensible conversation.

> 1 soft torpedo (hoagie, grinder, or submarine)
> roll

1 teaspoon, or more, extra-virgin olive oil
1 teaspoon, or more, balsamic vinegar (or another vinegar)
3 slices turkey, either pre-packaged or leftover home-cooked
3 slices capicola ham
3 slices prosciutto
3 slices Italian or Genoa salami
3 slices smoked ham
3 slices provolone cheese
4 slices tomato
3 heaping scoops jarred hot or sweet peppers, or both
Lettuce (optional)
Pinch of dried oregano
Pinch of dried parsley (or a fresh parsley sprig)
Fresh basil leaves

1. Split the roll open just like you see them do in any good sandwich shop.
2. Soak the roll with olive oil and then the vinegar.
3. Place the slices of meat on the roll. Top with the cheese, and then the tomatoes. Spoon the peppers on top.
4. Add lettuce, if you like, and sprinkle with the oregano and parsley, then add the fresh basil. Drizzle with just a hint more of olive oil and vinegar.
5. Close the sandwich, place it on a serving plate, and press down on the sandwich to meld the flavors. Cut the sandwich in half, or into sections, and serve to yourself and/or friends.

Makes 1 sandwich

Turkey Chili Sandwich on a Bun

If you like a decadent sloppy Joe as your guilty pleasure but, after listening to tales of cattle mutilation on *Coast,* you are thinking twice about beef, not to worry. Help is on the way. Rather than think twice, put your mind at ease and make your chili-flavored sloppy Joe with turkey instead. This is a perfect leftover turkey recipe.

Basic Turkey Chili

> 3 teaspoons olive oil
> 1 garlic clove, sliced
> 1 pound cooked turkey, cubed
> 1 bell pepper, seeded and finely diced
> 1 small white or red onion, finely diced
> Two 16-ounce cans whole or peeled tomatoes or
>   Italian plum tomatoes
> 2 large ripe fresh tomatoes
> 1 cup cold water or tomato juice
> 1 small hot pepper, chopped (optional)
> 2 tablespoons chili powder
> 1 teaspoon ground cumin or whole cumin seed
> 2 tablespoons dried oregano
> 1 teaspoon celery seed
> 1 teaspoon cayenne pepper or paprika
> 3 to 4 drops Tabasco or your favorite hot sauce
> Salt and freshly ground black pepper
> Two 8-ounce cans red pinto beans (optional)

1. In a large skillet over medium heat, slowly heat 2 teaspoons of the olive oil, add half of the sliced garlic, and cook, stirring, until fragrant. Add the turkey and brown it slowly until reheated.

2. Add the bell pepper and onion and cook, stirring occasionally, until the onion is nicely browned and the pepper softened. Simmer over very low heat for at least 10 minutes so the flavors cook through.

3. In a large stew pot, heat 1 teaspoon of the olive oil and add the remaining garlic. When the garlic starts to brown, add all the tomatoes and heat through. Cook for about 30 minutes, then add the peppers, onions, and turkey mixture. Mix through and add a cup of water or tomato juice and the hot pepper, if using.

4. Simmer over medium-low heat for at least 30 minutes, then add the chili, cumin, oregano, celery seed, cayenne or paprika, Tabasco, and salt and pepper to taste.

5. Simmer for at least an hour before you taste and adjust the spices because it will take that long for the spices to come up to their maximum level of flavor and mellow out. A mistake most novices make is to adjust the chili powder, cumin, and hot sauce levels too early so the chili mixture becomes too hot to eat. Take your time and wait an hour before adjusting to taste.

6. Depending on whether you want your chili to be a sloppy Joe–style sauce with beans, and how soft you want the beans, you can add the beans while waiting for the spices to percolate through the chili. Or you can wait until a half hour before you remove the chili from the heat.

7. Cook at a low simmer for at least another 1½ hours, preferably 2 hours.

8. Serve your turkey chili straight up, over rice, over noodles, or over a hamburger bun for a turkey chili sloppy Joe.

A pot of turkey chili easily serves 6 to 8 people, depending on the size of the servings and whether it is served as a sloppy Joe–style sauce for a turkey burger (see variation below) or on its own. Whether or not you add beans to the recipe also affects the size of the servings.

NOTE   You can replace the bell pepper and onion with frozen minced bell pepper and onion if you like. Likewise, you can replace the garlic clove with either store-bought garlic spread, dried garlic flakes, or even powdered garlic. However, I prefer fresh garlic in all recipes that call for garlic.

VARIATIONS   You can also use the chili sloppy Joe as a topping for a turkey burger, which is simple to make, either skillet-fried, oven-broiled, or grilled over charcoal or an open fire. You can also use precooked and frozen turkey burgers from the store and just heat them up in a microwave. Place the turkey burger on a bun, white or whole wheat, seeded or not, or even on a soft kaiser roll, and top with the turkey chili.

For another variation, instead of building your sandwich on a roll, bun, or even a torpedo roll, try your favorite type of bagel: garlic, sesame, poppy, or onion. If you can get fresh bagels from the supermarket or the local bagel bakery, you can serve your sloppy Joe–style turkey chili over bagels for lunch or a light dinner, or over a turkey burger. A toasted bagel holds up better under the intensity of the turkey chili, while a fresh bagel is probably better for a chili-topped turkey burger.

Fun Dates: The Webmaster's Delight

Ever had a fun date? No, not that kind of date, a date that is fun to eat because of a recipe you've made from it. Here's a recipe for dates, which become great late-night snacks you can actually have fun with. As with some of our previous recipes, if you have kids, and your kids like dates—and who doesn't—you'll find that even though this is a somewhat complicated recipe, it is well worth the effort because it's a late-night snack or treat that keeps on giving.

1 teaspoon butter
1¾ cups confectioners' sugar
2 tablespoons frozen orange juice concentrate
½ cup store-bought white frosting
15 pitted dates

1. Soften the butter in a microwave-safe cup or bowl on high for 90 seconds.
2. Add the sugar to the butter and stir through.
3. Add the orange juice concentrate, stir through, and microwave on the lowest setting for 1 minute; you are blending and softening, not boiling.
4. Remove the mixture from the microwave while still warm and shape into long, thin strings.
5. Cut the long strings of the confection mixture into short lengths and press into each of the pitted dates. You will have to cut as many short lengths as you have dates. Roll the stuffed dates in the white frosting. See how exciting this recipe is getting?
6. Microwave the frosted dates for 1 minute on the lowest setting. Serve while still warm. Alternatively, refrigerate the frosted dates for 15 minutes and serve chilled. Again, alternatively, especially in the summer, freeze, rather than refrigerate, the dates and serve them as summer snacks on those hot late nights when you and your friends are engrossed in what one of my guests is saying and then suddenly realize you need a taste explosion.

7. If the dates get too hard or stale, you can refresh them by heating them in your microwave for 1 minute on its lowest setting.

Makes 2 to 4 servings depending on how many dates you eat at one sitting

Didn't I tell you this was an exciting recipe? I don't have to hype my own stuff. All I have to do is lay this out, suggest you follow these directions for yourself, and, if you want to do me a favor, call me up on open lines to tell me how you enjoyed it.

11

• ETs • UFOs • UAPs •

Legend has it that aliens from outer space happen to have a predilection for strawberry ice cream. The reasons why have been lost to history, but we preserve that myth right here with several recipes involving strawberries.

Another legend suggests that a spaceship landed in a rural location one fine day and when the occupants encountered a farmer, they offered him pancakes. Why? Again, we'll never know, but in honor of that story we present a nice collection of pancakes, including ones with berries, of course.

Rounding things out, we have recipes for things that are round. It's only fair.

Banana Oatmeal Pancakes

Before you go bananas, if there is a diminutive occupant from a UFO knocking on your front door, just know that you can whip up some of these superior discs and he will go away happy and fulfilled.

1½ cups whole milk
⅓ cup (½ stick plus 1 tablespoon) butter, plus
    more for serving with pancakes
1½ cups quick-cooking oats
⅓ cup unsifted all-purpose flour
1½ teaspoons baking powder
½ teaspoon salt
1 tablespoon sugar
¼ teaspoon ground cinnamon
2 large eggs, separated
2 ripe bananas, diced
Confectioners' sugar, or berry or maple syrup,
    for serving

1. Slowly heat the milk and butter until the butter melts.
2. Remove from the heat, and stir in the oats. Set aside to cool.
3. In a separate bowl, stir together the flour, baking powder, salt, sugar, and cinnamon.
4. Add the egg yolks to the mixture, and stir just until blended.
5. In a separate bowl, beat the egg whites until stiff. Fold with the bananas into the mixture in the first bowl.
6. Drop spoonfuls of the pancake batter onto a greased skillet over medium-high heat. As each pancake forms bubbles on the top, lift with a wooden spoon (if you have a Teflon-coated

skillet, or flat spatula on a regular skillet) to check the underside for doneness. When just a light brown, flip the pancakes over and cook for a minute or two, checking the undersides to make sure they aren't burning. As each pancake is done, transfer from the skillet to serving plates, where you can top each one with a small pat of butter. Top with confectioners' sugar, berry syrup, or your favorite brand of maple syrup.

Makes 16 pancakes

Bagel Chips

Here's a very versatile snack that doubles as a breakfast treat, lunch treat, and as the perfect dip platform for hummus, guacamole, whipped cream cheese with smoked salmon, or even just good old salsa.

You can use any type of day-old bagel you like, cinnamon-raisin bagels for a dessert treat, onion or garlic bagels to get you started for the day, or some fabulously salted bagels for a late-night *Coast to Coast* snack.

After all, what's better for listening to Bruce Maccabee or Lynne Kitei talking about missing time captured on film than some nice salty bagel chips. Crunching them late at night is a real enjoyable snack. Moreover, not only are bagel chips snappy and delicious, they are a great way to use up bagels past their prime rather than leaving them out for the birds and squirrels.

Just use bagels that have not yet turned to cement. Those types of bagels you use for bagel horseshoe tosses, laminated refrigerator magnets, or doorstops. While you can still slice the bagels, here's how to make your own bagel chips:

3 to 6 old bagels, not hardened and still able to
   be split
⅛ to ¼ cup vegetable oil, depending on how
   many bagels you are making
2 tablespoons garlic salt or 1 tablespoon kosher
   salt mixed with 1 tablespoon garlic powder

1. Slice the bagels crosswise into very, very thin slices and arrange on a microwave-safe tray.
2. Using a pastry brush, lightly coat each bagel slice on both sides with vegetable oil.
3. Sprinkle both sides of each slice with garlic salt or the kosher salt and garlic powder mix.
4. Microwave for 5 minutes on medium, turn over and rotate, and microwave for 3 minutes on medium, making sure that both sides of each slice are nice and crisp. You can let cool for a bit and then wrap up what you're not going to eat right on the spot.

Makes 12 to 15 bagel chips

VARIATION   I'm starting off with the assumption that you're using plain bagels, but that need not be the case. If you are particularly enamored with cinnamon-raisin bagels, these make great chips, too, especially if you spread them as they come hot out of your microwave with straight cream cheese or cream cheese and chives.

That, plus a cup of green tea, is a wonderful late-night radio-time snack to tide you over until breakfast. Then have more bagel chips at breakfast, making sure to save some for the kids' lunch boxes as snacks.

Quick Mabel, the Pancakes!

You can make the basic ingredients—the biscuit mix and the chocolate sauce—any time so that you can always welcome any visitors with pancakes, as is the custom in some parts of the galaxy.

Use your Biscuit Baking Mix as the basis for these delicious pancakes, and then vary them by following some of the suggestions, here. You can top your pancakes with a sweet butter (page 192), or Sweet Berry Syrups (page 203), or simply top with Homemade Yogurt (page 42) for a lower-calorie treat.

> 2 cups Biscuit Baking Mix (page 29)
> 1 cup whole milk
> 2 large eggs

1. Combine all of the ingredients in a blender, food processor, or bowl, and beat until smooth. For thinner pancakes, use 1 egg and 1½ cups whole milk.
2. For each pancake, pour a small amount of batter into a hot, greased pan and cook over medium heat until bubbles form on the top. Flip and cook until the pancake is golden brown.

Chocolate Pancakes

> 2 cups Biscuit Baking Mix (page 29)
> ¾ cup whole milk
> ¼ cup Basic Chocolate Sauce (page 176)
> 1 large egg

Combine all of the ingredients and cook, as for Quick Mabel, the Pancakes! Top with sweet butter, sweetened whipped cream, or nuts.

Berry Pancakes

> 2 cups Biscuit Baking Mix (page 29)
> ¾ cup whole milk
> ½ cup fresh berries and juice
> 1 large egg

Combine all of the ingredients and cook, as for Quick Mabel, the Pancakes! Top with Sweet Butter (page 193), Sweet Berry Syrups (page 203), sweetened whipped cream, or nuts.

Each recipe makes 12 to 15 pancakes

Turkey Meatballs

Sure, you can buy them frozen in the supermarket. They're easy to defrost, microwave, and squeeze into a sandwich. But think of how much fresher and more personalized your own turkey meatballs can be, eaten right away or cooked, frozen, and saved for a variety of meals from basic spaghetti and turkey balls to mini turkey balls in gravy, to a heroic turkey ball sandwich on a torpedo roll with sauce, and melted cheese topped with a smidge of oregano and parsley.

Ready for a nice sandwich like this while listening to Stan Friedman, my buddy Richard Hoagland, or Steve Quayle expound on *Coast*? Sound tempting enough to entice you to try to make your own? Here's how:

1 tablespoon olive oil

1 garlic clove, thinly sliced, or more if desired

1 pound fresh ground turkey

½ cup Italian seasoned bread crumbs

1 teaspoon dried oregano

1 teaspoon dried parsley

1 teaspoon garlic powder

Pinch of crushed red pepper flakes (optional)

Salt and freshly ground black pepper

½ cup grated Parmesan or Romano cheese

1 large egg

¼ cup marinara sauce with basil or 8 ounces
   turkey gravy

1. Preheat the oven to 360°F.
2. Add the olive oil and the sliced garlic to a shallow baking dish and place in the oven to warm as the oven preheats.
3. In a medium bowl, knead the ground turkey, gradually, with the bread crumbs until blended.
4. Add the oregano, parsley, garlic powder, and red pepper flakes, if using. Season with salt and pepper. Add the grated cheese, then add the egg and knead the turkey mixture gently until the ingredients are well combined and the mixture is bound with the egg. Add the tomato sauce or turkey gravy and knead again to blend thoroughly.
5. Take small pieces of the meat mixture and roll them in the palms of your hands until you've formed them into balls of the size you want. If you are planning to serve cocktail-size turkey balls in turkey gravy, roll small balls. If you are making meatballs for either a pasta dish or a meatball sandwich, make them larger (approximately 1 inch in diameter). Set the meatballs aside on a plate as you form them.

6. When all of the turkey meat has been rolled into balls, place them in the baking dish in the oven and bake for at least 45 minutes, turning them frequently in the hot olive oil. You can add more olive oil, if needed, but be very careful of splattering.

7. After 30 minutes check for doneness to make sure you don't overcook the meatballs. Continue to cook as needed. Remove from the oven after 45 minutes and check again for doneness by splitting open 1 or 2 balls. Remove from the oven and use for your favorite turkey ball recipe.

Makes about 15 cocktail-size meatballs or 6 large meatballs

Peanut Butter Bananas

Foods are foods, snacks are snacks, but grazing separates the multitaskers from the herd. Like the weird night-creature we all are, I like to graze, whether at a tapas bar in LA or on my way back to my St. Louis studio in Missouri. But sometimes, when I have the time, I will prepare my own grazing guilty pleasures to stash away in my freezer for when they're needed.

6 firm bananas
12 wooden sticks or Popsicle sticks
6 tablespoons Homemade Peanut Butter (page 194)
½ cup Sweetened Condensed Milk (page 204)
Chopped nuts or crunchy cereal

1. Cut the bananas in half crosswise and place a wooden stick in each half.
2. Mix the peanut butter and milk until the mixture is smooth. Roll the bananas first in the milk mixture and then in the nuts or crunchy cereal. Cover with plastic wrap and freeze until firm.

Makes 12 banana pops

Fruity Italian Ices

I can remember the Italian ices truck when I was growing up in the neighborhoods of Detroit. The kids would see a truck on a hot summer day and stop whatever they were doing, sandlot baseball or even Little League games.

These ices would melt in minutes right over the ridged edges of the paper cups, get all over your hands to make them sticky—always helping out the pitchers—and you'd have to wipe them on your dungarees to clean them off. You would get yelled at for that. But who cared? Italian ices bring back my fondest of memories.

Try these on a warm summer's night as a pick-me-up for listening to *Coast*. In fact, if these bring back memories for you, call me on open lines and tell me about it.

You can eat these ices right from the paper cups you've frozen them in, squeezing it up in the cup as the ice melts, or you can freeze them in small plastic cups and eat with a small wooden or plastic spoon.

4 cups water
2 cups sugar

2 cups fresh orange juice
Juice of 2 lemons

1. Combine the water and sugar in a pan and bring to a boil. Boil for 5 minutes over medium heat, stirring occasionally. Set aside to cool.
2. Stir in the juices and pour the mixture into a freezer pan, ice cube tray, or a 9-inch cake pan and freeze for 30 minutes.
3. Remove the ice from the freezer, stir thoroughly, and return to the freezer. Repeat the process after 30 minutes.
4. Remove the mixture from the freezer, stir again, and press the ice into paper cups. Cover the tops of the cups with plastic wrap and freeze until firm.

Makes 10 ices

VARIATIONS   Try substituting the juice of another fruit for the orange juice, and retaining the lemon juice in the recipe. Raspberry, pineapple, and grape juice ices are delicious.

Quickie Ice Cream

Because all memories are connected, neurologically as well as cognitively, immediately I am reminded of the taste of homemade chocolate ice cream. I can imagine the first hit of chocolate, and like Monsieur Swann in Marcel Proust's *Remembrance of Things Past,* a swirl of childhood events, sounds, and images floods my mind.

Have you had experiences like that, where you taste something, like ice cream or a special treat, and you are transported back in your mind to an event you associate with that treat?

This chocolate ice cream is a little quirky—it's not a traditional ice cream, but it's not bad, either. If you don't have an ice cream maker, here is one to try with just a freezer compartment as the basic equipment needed.

⅔ cup Basic Chocolate Sauce (page 176)
2 cups Sweetened Condensed Milk (page 204)
1 cup heavy cream, whipped

1. In a large saucepan, combine the sauce and condensed milk and fold in the whipped cream. Pour the mixture into a freezer tray, a 9-inch cake pan, or an ice cube tray and freeze for 30 minutes.
2. Pour the mushy mixture into a blender or whip with an electric mixer for 1 minute. Pour back into the tray, cover with plastic wrap, and freeze until firm.

Makes 32 ounces ice cream

VARIATIONS   Instead of chocolate sauce, try adding ⅔ cup of Freezer Fruit Preserves (page 60), or add ½ cup chocolate chips and 1 teaspoon mint extract to the chocolate recipe.

Instant Ice Cream

Try this treat if you have an antsy child around, or if you feel antsy yourself. The way the mixture changes to ice cream right before your very eyes is very involving and exciting, and of course you must eat the frozen concoction right away or the magic will be lost.

½ cup Homemade Yogurt (page 42)

2 large egg whites

3 tablespoons sugar

2 teaspoons lemon juice

3 cups frozen fruit in small pieces

1. If you have time, chill the blender container by placing it in the freezer for about 10 minutes before beginning.
2. Place the yogurt, egg whites, sugar, and juice in the blender and blend for 1 minute. Keep the machine running and gradually add the frozen fruit until soft ice cream is formed. Serve at once.

Makes 24 ounces ice cream

Strawberry Ice Cream Lures

This is a special version of the alien's favorite strawberry ice cream. Maybe you'll be able to tell the humans from the aliens with this hybrid.

⅔ cup Homemade Cream Cheese (page 44), softened

1 cup Sweetened Condensed Milk (page 204)

⅓ cup heavy cream

1 cup sugar

2 teaspoons finely grated lemon zest

1½ cups fresh strawberries

1. Mix the cream cheese, milk, cream, sugar, and zest until well blended. Freeze for 4 hours or until almost solid.

2. Using an electric mixer, beat the frozen cream cheese mixture until creamy.
3. Blend the berries in a blender until smooth. Add to the cream cheese mixture and combine well. Freeze for 8 hours or until firm.

Makes about 2 cups ice cream

How About a Crisp?

For a city boy, nothing seems more alien than rhubarb, but it's quite good—tart, yes—when combined with strawberries. Try it! You might like it.

8 ounces strawberries, hulled and halved
8 ounces rhubarb, trimmed, cut into ½-inch
**   pieces**
½ cup sugar
1 tablespoon cornstarch
¼ teaspoon coarse salt, plus ⅛ teaspoon
1 cup rolled oats
¼ cup all-purpose flour
¼ cup (½ stick) unsalted butter, melted
¼ cup packed brown sugar
Fresh basil leaves, for garnish (optional)

1. Preheat the oven to 375°F.
2. In a large bowl, combine the strawberries, rhubarb, sugar, cornstarch, and ¼ teaspoon salt. Transfer to an 8-inch baking dish.

3. In a medium bowl, combine the oats, flour, butter, brown sugar, and remaining salt. Stir until combined and slightly clumpy. Sprinkle over the fruit.
4. Bake the crisp until the juices are bubbling in the center and the topping is golden brown, about 45 minutes. Let cool slightly. Garnish with fresh basil, if you want to complete the great taste, and serve with vanilla ice cream or crème fraîche.

Makes one 8 by 8-inch crisp

Berry Berry Honey Butter

1 pint strawberries, hulled
1 pint raspberries
3 tablespoons honey
2 teaspoons fresh lemon juice, or to taste
¾ cup (1½ sticks) unsalted butter, softened

1. In a food processor, gently puree the strawberries and transfer to a saucepan. Add the pint of raspberries.
2. Add the honey and the lemon juice and boil the mixture, stirring, for 3 minutes, or until it has thickened. Set aside and cool to room temperature.
3. In a separate bowl, cream together the butter and berry mixture. Let the mixture stand, covered, in a cool place for 1 hour to allow the flavors to develop.

Makes 8 ounces butter

Marinated Mushrooms

I've always liked this dish as a happy lunch, a late breakfast with eggs, a dinner appetizer, or a late-night snack. You can make this in advance, let it sit in the fridge, and enjoy it whenever the mood strikes or your favorite guest is on *Coast*.

The type of oil you use in this recipe can change the taste of the final marinade as well as change the price. It doesn't hurt to try the recipe with regular vegetable oil because the addition of several spices and the mustard will help to spruce up the flavor.

A high-quality olive oil is the way to make this recipe special, and costly, but if you're giving it as a gift, it will still save you money over the gourmet brands in specialty stores.

> 2 cups fresh mushrooms
> 1 cup vegetable oil
> ½ cup red wine vinegar
> 3 garlic cloves, chopped
> 2 tablespoons chopped fresh parsley
> 1 teaspoon Tangy Mustard (page 201)
> ½ teaspoon dried rosemary
> ¼ teaspoon dried thyme
> ¼ teaspoon dried oregano

1. Clean the mushrooms by rinsing them gently under running water, patting them dry with paper towels, and trimming off the tough stems.
2. Place all of the ingredients, except the mushrooms, in a sterilized glass jar. Cover and shake well to mix. Drop in the mushrooms, making sure they are completely covered with the liquid, and marinate overnight. The mushrooms will keep, refrigerated, for 2 to 4 months.

Makes 16 ounces marinated mushrooms

VARIATIONS   The marinade is good for other vegetables, especially as you use some of the mushrooms up and find yourself
with a supply of seasoned marinade on hand. Try dropping in
onion slices or strips of green bell pepper for a different tasting
combination.

You can also add artichoke hearts that are canned in water.
Drain them for 10 minutes on paper towels before adding them
to the marinade. I've added blanched green beans to the marinade, as well as cauliflower.

Richard Hoagland's Donut Delites

Whether or not there's a face on Mars is one issue. But there is
certainly a smile on Richard Hoagland's face when he thinks
of these donut delites. For sure, if the convenience store is too
far away to run out to for a nice doughnut, or if the doughnut
shops near you are all closed, or if you simply want to stay
home in your robe and don't want to get in the car on a howling windy and snowy night, you'll find solace right here and
right now.

I have come up with the solution, which, while no fresh
Krispy Kreme, can save all of us from doughnut deprivation. It's
simple, buy as many packages of doughnuts as you want, make
sure your microwave is ready for the task, and keep the following ingredients on hand.

Store-bought or bakery plain doughnuts
½ cup of each of the following:
   Peanut butter
   Marshmallow Fluff

Maraschino cherries
Milk chocolate squares
Chopped Heath bars
Shredded coconut

1. Place the individual doughnuts on a flat microwave-safe sheet and top with one or more, in any combination, of the above ingredients.
2. Microwave on the lowest power setting until the toppings melt.

There are some things in this world you don't even have to think about. Top 'em, bake 'em, and eat 'em. Done and down in under a few minutes, and nothing could be simpler.

Makes 12 to 24 Donut Delites

Old-Time Doughnuts

Remember the television commercial where a beleaguered, but affable, man awakens in the middle of the night to announce, "Time to make the doughnuts"? I do. It inspired me to learn how to make my own doughnuts.

I made them for my friends, too, who to this day remember eating these doughnuts, brushed with confectioners' sugar, at Christmas. You can make up some of your own memories with these doughnuts on a cold, blowy winter night.

Serve them while they are still toasty warm, with hot mulled cider or hot chocolate. Make them in advance, refrigerate them, and heat them up in the middle of the night for a luxurious evening with my guests on the radio.

DOUGHNUTS

2 large eggs

1 cup granulated sugar

2 tablespoons vegetable shortening

¾ cup buttermilk

3½ cups sifted all-purpose flour

2 teaspoons baking powder

1 teaspoon baking soda

½ teaspoon salt

1 teaspoon ground cinnamon

½ teaspoon ground nutmeg

Cooking oil

COATING

½ cup Cinnamon-Sugar (page 181)

½ cup confectioners' sugar or Powdered Vanilla
  Sugar (page 180)

1. Using a food processor or an electric mixer, beat the eggs
   until they are light and fluffy. Beat in the granulated sugar
   and shortening. Stir in the buttermilk.
2. Sift the flour, baking powder, baking soda, salt, and spices
   into a bowl. Stir into the egg mixture until well combined.
3. Turn the dough out onto a floured surface and knead gently 4 or 5 times. Roll the dough out to a thickness of ⅓ inch.
   Let the dough rest for 30 minutes.
4. Cut out doughnut shapes with a doughnut cutter, or flour
   and use the rims of two glasses: a drinking glass for the
   doughnuts and a shot glass for the holes.
5. Pour cooking oil into an electric skillet or deep, heavy-
   bottomed pan to a depth of 2 inches and heat the oil to
   375°F.

Old-time Doughnuts

6. Fry the doughnuts and holes until browned on one side; carefully turn and fry on the opposite side. Transfer the doughnuts to several layers of paper towels or place on clean brown paper bags to drain.

7. Pour the Cinnamon-Sugar and the confectioners' sugar into two separate brown lunch bags and drop the doughnuts into one or the other while still warm. Shake and serve.

Makes two dozen 3-inch doughnuts

NOTE   If you want to substitute plain milk for the buttermilk, increase the baking powder to 4 teaspoons and omit the baking soda.

Cream-Filled Chocolate Cookies

A cookie like this can cause a sort of obsessive behavior in certain people—they like to take it apart, eat the filling, and then dunk the rest of the cookie in milk. If you know any of those people, you might make a double batch of this cookie, or try adding a double dollop of filling. You can also add a teaspoon of jelly or a drop of mint extract to the filling.

Just imagine enjoying a batch of these cookies while listening to stories of crashed alien spacecraft in the depths of Lake Vostok, or alien devices discovered in secret by archeologists in dig sites with dinosaur bones. This is exactly the kind of information that generates the cookie-eating machine.

For more authentic-looking cookies, it's a nice idea to press a fancy design in the top layer of cookie with a butter mold or clean rubber stamp just before baking. Why not press the image of a flying saucer or the head of an alien? If you have friends over for a late-night listening and discussion session, these cookies are just the ticket.

COOKIES
¾ cup vegetable shortening
½ cup (1 stick) butter
2 cups granulated sugar
1 large egg
2½ cups all-purpose flour
½ cup unsweetened cocoa powder

FILLING
2 cups confectioners' sugar or Powdered Vanilla
   Sugar (page 180)
½ cup (1 stick) unsalted butter
2 tablespoons heavy cream
2 tablespoons Vanilla Bean Extract (page 205)

1. Using a food processor or an electric mixer, cream together the shortening and the butter. Gradually beat in the granulated sugar and the egg, beating well after each addition, until the mixture is light and lemon-colored.
2. Sift together the flour and cocoa and add to the creamed mixture, blending well.
3. Shape the dough into several rolls, each about 1 inch in diameter. Wrap the rolls in wax paper and refrigerate for several hours or overnight.
4. Preheat the oven to 375°F.
5. Unwrap and cut the rolls of cookie dough into ⅛-inch-thick slices. Place on ungreased baking sheets and bake for 5 to 8 minutes. Cool before adding the filling.
6. To make the filling, cream the confectioners' sugar and butter together. Add the cream and vanilla.

7. Create a cookie "sandwich" with two cookies and a generous dab of the filling. The cookies will keep for up to 2 weeks in a cookie jar, or for 4 to 5 months in the freezer.

Makes 24 to 36 cookies depending on the size of the dough drops

---

Plain and Fancy Fruiti Pops

Yes, I confess, I like ice-cream pops, Popsicles, or any kind of sweet on a pop. The smoother the better. The degree of smoothness you want in these pops is entirely your choice. If you are making the pops for very small children, try making a mixture that is on the smooth side; others might prefer a mixture with plenty of fruity chunks.

Plain Fruiti Pops

> **1 cup fresh, frozen, or canned fruit**
> **1 cup fruit juice**
> **10 Popsicle sticks**

1. Mix the fruit and fruit juice together in a blender or food processor. You can either puree the fruit completely or simply whirl the fruit and juice to mix thoroughly while still leaving some chunks.
2. Pour the mixture into molds or paper cups to freeze. Freeze until slightly firm, insert the sticks, and continue freezing until firm.

Makes 10 pops

Fruit 'n' Cream Pops

    1 cup fruit and its juice
    1 cup light cream or 1 cup whole milk mixed
       with ½ cup instant nonfat dry milk
    1 teaspoon honey
    ½ teaspoon Vanilla Bean Extract (page 205)
    10 Popsicle sticks
    1 cup Basic Chocolate Sauce (page 176) (optional)

1. Mix together the fruit and cream. Whip in the honey and vanilla until the fruit mixture is well blended.

2. Freeze in a freezer container or an ice cube tray for 40 minutes. Spoon the slightly frozen mixture into a blender or food processor and blend for 30 seconds. Pour the mixture into molds or paper cups, insert the sticks, and freeze until firm. After the pops are frozen solid, try swirling them in chocolate sauce and eating immediately.

Makes about 10 pops

Frosted Banana Pops

Here is another freezer goody that is also good for you. You can set out the ingredients and let your kids assemble these treats all by themselves.

    6 firm bananas
    12 Popsicle sticks
    1 cup Basic Chocolate Sauce (page 176)
    ½ cup shredded unsweetened coconut

1. Cut the bananas in half crosswise and place a wooden stick in each half.

2. Dip the bananas first in chocolate sauce and then in the coconut to cover. Wrap a plastic bag around each banana half, leaving the stick poking out. Use a twist tie to secure the bag around the stick, and freeze the bananas until firm, about 2 hours.

Makes 12 banana pops

Frozen Fruiti Yogurt Pops

I have to tell you I can't live without yogurt, especially when I get up in the morning after an intense night on *Coast* with a guest that gets your brain spinning. Imagine Richard Hoagland e-mailing you photos of something strange going on near a crater on Mars or one of those odd-looking shapes on the lunar surface. How can you grok that? You don't.

You only accept what you're looking at and hope that someone at JPL tells you it's just a shadow. Because if it's them and not us, somebody's got some explaining to do. So, after a night of wondering whether this is the real evidence, I wake up and need something to jump-start the day. That, for me, is yogurt.

If you are making up a nice batch of creamy Homemade Yogurt (page 42), you will undoubtedly have enough on hand to turn into frozen fruit-flavored yogurt pops.

> 2 cups plain Homemade Yogurt (page 42)
> 1 cup fresh or frozen fruit: banana, orange,
>   strawberries, raspberries, or a combination
> ¼ cup honey
> 10 to 20 Popside sticks, depending on the size of
>   the pops.

1. Puree the yogurt and fruit in a blender, adding the honey once the fruit is well blended.
2. Pour the mixture into a freezer container: an ice cube tray, a shallow plastic container, or a 9-inch-square cake pan. Freeze for 30 minutes.
3. Spoon the frozen mush into a blender container and blend for 1 minute. Pour the mixture into molds or paper cups. Freeze for 10 minutes, insert the sticks, and return to the freezer until firm.

Makes 20 ounces Fruiti Yogurt

VARIATIONS   Spices and other flavorings can be added as you experiment with fruit and yogurt combinations. For example, try ½ teaspoon vanilla, ½ teaspoon ground cinnamon, and ½ teaspoon ground nutmeg whipped up with 1 banana.

Or, try mixing 6 ounces frozen juice concentrate with 1 cup yogurt and 1 teaspoon vanilla.

12

• WEIRD • BIZARRE •

Sneaky Coleslaw
Silly Sparkles
Sugared Flowers
Sugared Almonds
Sugared Pecans
Candied Citrus Peel
Holiday Fruitcake
Mustard Mayonnaise

Here's where we put the recipes that are fun but nonetheless bizarre. Can you eat flowers? Sure, but be careful and make sure there are no Mad Hatters lurking about before you indulge.

Hunkering down late at night to listen to *Coast* is what I imagine most people do. However, folks have told me that when we have a special guest breaking a big story, such as Lloyd Pye telling us about the DNA of the Starchild Skull, folks in my listening audience like to make it a party.

Here are some recipes for just such a party and for party gifts folks can take home with them, special gifts from me to you and your friends. It's pretty much a mixed bag here, but all very snazzy and schmaltzy nevertheless.

And why do fruitcakes last forever? Why are they so polarizing? Celebrate your inner fruitcake with our version here.

Sneaky Coleslaw

Here is a stealthy way to get some vegetables into yourself and your loved ones. You can hardly taste the vitamins in the zucchini, and you know you're going to have extra zucchini to get rid of some time this year.

So, pull a fast one and make a delicious, healthy, and stealthy treat. After all, it is merely a side dish, not too hard to swallow.

> 2 cups shredded zucchini
> 1 cup shredded carrot
> ¼ cup whole milk
> ¼ cup buttermilk
> ½ cup mayonnaise
> 1 teaspoon Dijon mustard
> ⅓ cup sugar
> 1 tablespoon lemon juice
> 1 tablespoon apple cider vinegar
> 1 tablespoon poppy seeds
> Salt and freshly ground black pepper

1. Place the shredded zucchini in a colander and let drain thoroughly, about 30 minutes.
2. Toss the drained zucchini with the shredded carrot in a large salad bowl.
3. In a separate bowl, whisk together the milk, buttermilk, mayonnaise, and mustard.
4. Add the sugar, lemon juice, and vinegar. Add the poppy seeds, and season with salt and pepper to taste.
5. Pour the dressing over the vegetables in the salad bowl and toss to coat.

6. Chill the coleslaw for 1 hour to allow the flavors to meld. Remove from the refrigerator, stir, taste, and correct the seasonings, if needed.

Makes 2 cups coleslaw

Silly Sparkles

To make these colored sugars, choose familiar edible substances for colors over flowers or herbs, which are best left for coloring craft items. For example, dyes made from beets, cabbage, berries, onion skins, or spinach are preferable to those made from grass, moss, or coffee grounds.

Choose the colors you like and don't worry about the flavors mixing with the sugar. Once all the liquid or juice from the flavor has evaporated, the sugar will still taste like sugar. Or, just use regular food coloring in place of natural colors.

> 3 cups sugar
> 1 cup food coloring, diluted in 2 cups water

1. Preheat the oven to 150°F.
2. Stir together the sugar and dye and spread the mixture out on a shallow baking pan. Place the sugar in the oven for 20 minutes, stirring every 5 minutes. Remove when the liquid has evaporated. Set aside to cool.
3. Store the sugar in a tightly covered jar or airtight container.

Makes 24 ounces Silly Sparkles

Sugared Flowers

Here is a real grandpa's recipe for surprising the kids on their birthdays or just about anytime they come over on a weekend. I make 'em up and store them so if I either make cupcakes or buy them at the supermarket, I can decorate them with sugared flowers for a real surprise. The kids love it.

Try making and carefully storing some of these beautiful blossoms and you will never again wonder how to finish off a special cake or dessert. The flowers are sweet, beautiful, and ready to eat. Violets have always been the traditional flower to sugar, but you can also try tiny rosebuds or just the rose petals.

It would help to assemble all your supplies and ingredients before beginning this recipe, because you should work quickly and with a delicate touch. You will need a small paintbrush and a parchment paper–covered wire rack for drying.

> ½ cup sugar
> 1 large egg white
> Freshly picked pesticide-free blossoms, with
>   stems

1. Place the sugar in a blender or food processor and process until the sugar is a fine powder. Pour the sugar into a shallow bowl and set aside.
2. Beat the egg white until foamy and pour into a shallow bowl. Paint each of the flower blossoms carefully with the egg white, sprinkle with the sugar powder, and carefully lay on the parchment paper–covered rack to dry. The flowers will dry in the positions you arrange them, so be careful to spread out the petals. Sprinkle with a bit more sugar.

3. Dry the flowers in a sunny spot, or you can preheat your oven to 200°F, turn it off, and place the flowers inside to dry with the door left open.

4. Carefully remove the completely dried flowers and layer them, nestled on tissue paper, in a box. The flowers will keep for 6 to 9 months in a cool, dry place.

TO USE Place the flowers on cupcakes for your grandchildren.

Or make Violets in the Snow: whip heavy cream with 1 teaspoon vanilla, 1 teaspoon finely grated orange zest, and 1 teaspoon sugar until stiff. Dot with the violets and serve.

Makes 8 ounces sugared blossoms, about 8 flowers

Sugared Almonds

Did you know that almonds are one of the perfect superfoods that control bad cholesterol? It's true. Just two almonds a day go a long way to lowering bad cholesterol, LDL, and when combined with a nice green veggie drink, keep your entire system in tune. Now, I like to add sugar to my almond snacks for an energy shot during the show.

A jar of these snacking treats can also be a welcome gift to someone who can use a little comforting. If you prefer, other nuts, such as hazelnuts or macadamia nuts, can be substituted for the almonds.

1 cup sugar
1 cup honey
½ cup water

1 pound unblanched whole almonds
1 teaspoon ground cinnamon
1 teaspoon ground allspice

1. Mix the sugar, honey, and water in a heavy skillet, bring to a boil, and boil the mixture for 5 minutes, or until it is thick.
2. Add the nuts and cook until the nuts start to crackle. Sprinkle on the cinnamon and allspice, reduce the heat, and continue stirring until the mixture is dry.

Makes 1 pound sugared almonds

Sugared Pecans

Nuts that are sweet, salty, and spicy are pretty much the perfect snack.

1 pound pecan halves
⅓ cup (½ stick plus 1 tablespoon) butter or margarine
¼ cup sugar
½ teaspoon ground cinnamon
¼ teaspoon ground ginger

1. Preheat the oven to 275°F.
2. Spread the pecan halves out on a shallow baking pan. In a small saucepan, heat the butter, sugar, and spices until the butter melts. Pour the mixture over the pecans in the baking pan, making sure to coat all of the nuts.
3. Bake for 30 minutes, stirring several times during baking.

Cool and store in an airtight container. The nuts will keep well for 4 to 6 weeks.

Makes 32 ounces sugared pecans

Candied Citrus Peel

This is a happy candy snack you can put in a plastic bag and carry around for a refresher, pack along with your lunch for a long-lasting dessert, or, which is what I do, enjoy late at night. When I'm in front of the mike and take a break, I can slip one of these great citrus peels into my mouth and let it smooth out my voice, especially during a tough winter in St. Louis. And, best of all, you can put a lemon citrus peel into your cup of tea and enjoy the sweet flavor it imparts.

You can use any kind of citrus for this recipe, and a nice variety of peel will give you a good range of color and flavor. No matter what citrus you use—orange, lemon, lime, tangerine, grapefruit—remember to scrape away every trace of the white pith under the peel as it is very bitter.

> 2 cups citrus peel
> Water for boiling, plus ½ cup water
> 1 cup sugar, plus more for coating the peels

1. Wash and dry the fruit carefully before using. Remove the peel from the fruit using a vegetable peeler or a sharp paring knife. Trim away all of the white pith and cut the peel into narrow strips about 1 inch long.
2. Place the peels in a saucepan with 2 cups of water and simmer for 10 minutes. Drain, add 2 cups of fresh water, and

simmer for another 10 minutes. Repeat until the peels have been simmered and drained 4 separate times.

3. In a large saucepan, combine the sugar and ½ cup of water and bring to a boil. Boil for 1 minute and add the drained peel. Simmer gently until the peels have absorbed the liquid, about 20 minutes.

4. Spread the peels out on a rack to dry. Roll the candied peels in additional sugar and dry on sheets of wax paper or plastic wrap. When completely dry, store in an airtight container. The candied peels will keep for 2 to 4 months on the pantry shelf.

Makes 16 ounces candied peel

VARIATION   Peels are delicious dipped into Basic Chocolate Sauce (page 176) for a special treat.

Holiday Fruitcake

You'd be surprised about two things concerning fruitcakes. First, they keep forever, just like a Twinkie. I'm sure millions of years in the future when visitors from a distant star system land here to inspect the detritus of humanity, they'll find remnants of fruitcakes, scratch one of their many heads, and one of them will write its Ph.D. thesis on the symbolic significance of fruitcakes.

Second, they taste pretty good, which is why many folks like them so much even if it's not a holiday. I like them because you can make them up in advance, bring a slice or two with you to the studio, and feast on one during a long station break or during the news.

There are as many types of fruitcakes as there are nationalities of people celebrating the holidays with sweet cake. One of my favorites, and I like all of them, is a white fruitcake, which is attributed to Martha Washington. Here is my version of it.

Since this cake has to age and mellow, you should plan to make it well in advance of the holiday rush—it's a nice, rich, cozy way to welcome the first gray day of November.

> 1 cup golden raisins
> 1 cup chopped dried apricots
> ½ cup brandy, plus 1 cup for aging
> ½ pound candied orange peel (see page 280)
> ½ pound candied lemon peel (see page 280)
> ½ pound candied pineapple, chopped
> ¼ pound candied citron, chopped
> ¼ cup chopped walnuts
> 4½ cups all-purpose flour, sifted
> 1 teaspoon ground mace
> 1 teaspoon ground cinnamon
> 1 teaspoon ground allspice
> 1 teaspoon ground nutmeg
> 2 cups (4 sticks) butter
> 2 cups granulated sugar
> 1 cup lightly packed brown sugar
> 8 large eggs
> 2 tablespoons molasses
> ¼ cup dry sherry

1. One day before baking, mix together the raisins, apricots, and ½ cup of the brandy in a medium saucepan. Simmer for 5 minutes, remove from the heat, and let stand for 30 minutes.
2. Combine the raisin-apricot-brandy mixture with the orange and lemon peel, pineapple, citron, and walnuts. Toss to coat

Holiday Fruitcake

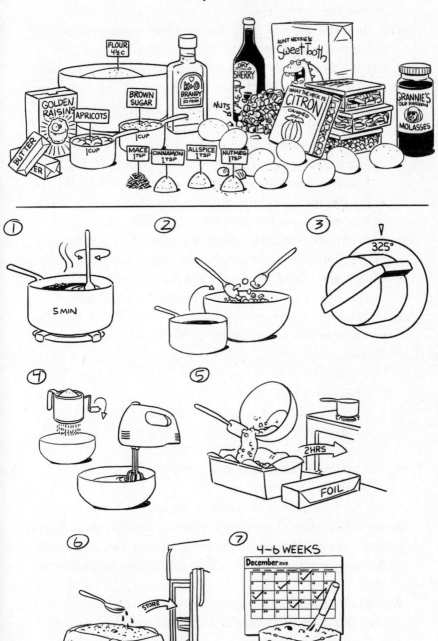

all the fruit and let the mixture stand at room temperature overnight.

3. Preheat the oven to 325°F. Grease a loaf pan and line with parchment paper, or grease a Bundt cake pan.

4. Sift together the flour and spices into a bowl. In a separate bowl, cream together the butter, sugars, and eggs until the mixture is light and fluffy. Stir in the molasses, sherry, and brandied fruits and nuts.

5. Pour the batter into the prepared pan. Bake for 2 hours, or until a cake tester inserted in the center comes out clean. If necessary, cover the cake with aluminum foil during baking to prevent excessive browning. Cool the cake on a wire rack, then remove the cake from the pan.

6. Wrap the cake in cheesecloth. Sprinkle 2 to 4 tablespoons of brandy on the cheesecloth and wrap tightly. Place in a thick layer of heavy-duty aluminum foil or in an airtight tin. Store in a cool, dry place or in the refrigerator.

7. Once every 5 days, unwrap the cake, brush with brandy, and rewrap and store. Continue this aging process for 4 to 6 weeks.

Makes 1 fruitcake

Mustard Mayonnaise

Which is it? Mustard or mayo? That's where the mystery lies, of course. If you were to combine ketchup and mayo, you'd have Russian dressing. It is not necessary to purchase expensive Dijonnaise when you can make your own quick and easy schmear.

    3 to 4 tablespoons regular or light mayonnaise
    2 teaspoons spicy mustard or Dijon mustard

1 to 2 drops Tabasco or your favorite hot sauce
Pinch of ground, dried, or chopped fresh parsley

Combine all of the ingredients in a small bowl until thoroughly blended and spread on your sandwich.

Makes ½ cup mustard mayonnaise

Final Words

These are my absolute favorite treats. I've tried to make them simple to prepare. No gourmet stuff here. Just plain and simple guilty pleasures to sustain you as you wend your way through the maze of the paranormal, challenging your very concept of reality. To the radio hosts who have come before me, Long John Nebel, the famous Barry Farber, the pioneering Art Bell, and others on late-night radio shows around the country who dare broach the concept that there is more to the world than we can actually see, I tip my s'more.

To my great and fearless guests over the years. To the ageless Stan Friedman and meticulous Bruce Maccabee or the fighting Woods, champions of the MJ-12 documents. To the late Betty and Barney Hill as well as to our 1950s contactee forebears, I want to tell your stories and make sure my loyal listeners and callers-in are well cared for and well fed.

So when you see a lonely bag of popcorn on the store shelf, don't just think of it as a plain bag of popcorn, cheesed up or not. Think of it as the basis for a late-night treat that you will savor and save and keep on hand for nights to come, ready to welcome you to the paranormal world of *Coast to Coast*.

Call me. You know where to find me. My lines are always open.

Index